The Ten Commandments:

They Still Work!

Dr. Martin A. Case

The Ten Commandments: They Still Work
Dr. Martin A. Case

© 2001 by Mercy Press, P.O. Box 837, Batesville, MS 38606

Printed in the United States of America
ISBN 1-931232-18-0

Printed by Xulon Press
344 Maple Ave. West, #302
Vienna, VA 22180
703-691-7595
XulonPress.com

Table of Contents

About the Author

Dr. Martin Alexander Case has served in the ministries of the United Methodist Church since 1953. He graduated from Central High School in Jackson, Mississippi, in 1950 and attended two years at Millsaps College there before completing his bachelor's degree at Asbury College in Wilmore, Kentucky, in 1954. He received his bachelor's of divinity degree from Asbury Theological Seminary in 1957, did graduate work at Lutheran Seminary in Gettysburg, Pennsylvania, from 1965-1966, and was awarded an honorary doctorate from Wesley Biblical Seminary in Jackson, Mississippi, in 1988.

His career in the ministry took him to three conferences: the Kentucky Conference as a student from 1953-57, the Baltimore Conference from 1962-68, and the Mississippi Conference from 1957-62 and 1968-2000. He served in various capacities outside his own church as District Secretary of Evangelism, Conference Chairperson of Camping, District Superintendent, and Delegate to General Conference (1992 and 1996) and to Jurisdictional Conference (1992, 1996, and 2000).

He is the son of the late Reverend and Mrs. Robert E. Case, husband of Flora Elizabeth (Betty) Case, and father of two children: Donna and David. Donna is married to Tom Vickroy and they hae sons Aaron, Alex, and Nathan. David and his wife have daughters Elizabeth, Catherine, and Mary Madelon.

Dr. Case has authored three earlier publications, the first of which is still available through Disciple Resources: *Four Great Emphases of United Methodism*, *Our United Methodist Beliefs*, and *Our Stewardship*. He retired in June 2000 from the day-to-day duties as a local pastor and now makes his home with his wife Betty in Oxford, Mississippi. He remains active as a revival speaker, prayer workshop leader, author, and guest lecturer.

Acknowledgements

A great many people are owed gratitude for the encouragement provided for this volume. First, my thanks goes to the congregation of First United Methodist Church in Batesville, Mississippi, where the ideas of this book found initial expression in a series of fall sermons in 1999 in response to their expressed interest in a deeper understanding of the Ten Commandments. The enthusiasm during and after the series brought forward the inspiration for this material to be placed in book form. One member, Marni McKenzie, a long-time teacher for Explorer's Bible Study, put the plan into action. She enlisted her friend Sandy Jenkins to transcribe the sermon tapes into readable form, and then set in motion the longer task of editing and re-writing. That work was a cooperative effort for Marni and myself over several months. Marni's suggestions and retyping of the revisions were invaluable, plus her deep, insistent conviction that the Decalogue is just as much God's Word for people in this new millennium as it was for the people of ancient Israel. Good friends Betty Keating and Debbie Bowie gave many hours to the task of proofreading, for which I am grateful.

I owe much, of course, to many whose efforts have shed light on my understanding of the Ten Commandments. Dr. David Seamands, a long-time pastor at First United Methodist Church in Wilmore, Kentucky, home of Asbury College and Asbury

Theological Seminary, preached on the Ten Commandments, and his series challenged me. Dr. Clovis Chappel's book, *Ten Rules for Living*, stirred my interest in the Ten Commandments. Dr. J. Ellsworth Kalas deepened my own convictions about the relevance of the commandments for a world adrift from moral moorings in his book *The Ten Commandments from the Backside*. Finally, William Barclay's commentary in the *Wesley Study Bible* added helpful insights, too.

Foreword

The culture in which we Americans live, indeed, is a curious one. Eight out of every ten people in America profess to be of the Christian faith. The Declaration of Independence speaks definitively of a Creator who endows people with inalienable rights, yet one cannot publicly speak of the same Creator, nor make assertions about His existence without some purporting that it is a violation of United States law. In fact, as we press into a third millennium after Christ, many social historians say America is in the "post-Christian" era.

Dr. Thomas Oden, well known United Methodist theologian, has said in his book, *Agenda for Theology, After Modernity What?* that the watchword of this post-modern politic is tolerance. Strangely enough, to be intolerant is the greatest reproach of the age. Yet, there is little tolerance of a self-professed eighty percent majority who believe that Christian values must be lived out in every arena, not for the purpose of promoting religious ideology, but to live authentically —and if authentically, then in truth.

It is fair to say that there are some insidious dangers to being a practicing Christian in this culture. We are filled with self-doubt.

There are definite reasons for this. In the nineteenth century these particular challenges did not exist because Christianity was not dominated by the spirit of tolerance, but rather by the Spirit of Truth. Nowhere can these thoughts be more readily discerned than in our educational systems. At the turn of the nineteenth century, the better PhD programs in the country offered an advocacy to a discipline, and one chose where to study because there were extant schools of thought. Today the PhD is a professional degree, and embracing a particular advocacy is prohibitive. The essence of education then is to learn to investigate. It is intolerant to advocate.

It is little surprise to know that one hundred years ago the vast majority of theological schools saw the study of ethics as a mandatory part of seminary training. Today, however, less than ten percent of theological schools in America require ethics as a mandatory part of training clergy. Why? Ethics lay claim to mandatory, prescribed behaviors. But, the spirit of the times that drives the church and the culture in which it is housed is tolerance.

Perhaps the best illustration of my point took place after the Monica Lewinsky scandal in the Oval Office. Following a very emotional explanation that the scandal was precipitated by giving in to typical human passion, the nation was asked to forgive the Chief Executive. At the national prayer breakfast, a fairly well known American evangelical said this prayer: "The only difference between sinner and saint, is that one's got forgiveness and the other one ain't [sic]." The tenor of the Christianity coming from Capitol Hill was unmistakable. The real issue was forgiveness, and the real culprit was intolerance. On that day, publicly in America, truth became suspect, and ethics backslid. Tolerance was promoted, even at the expense of a God who was desperately yearning for a Biblical advocate analogous to Paul the Apostle who could have stepped forward and said, "Those who belong to Christ have crucified the flesh along with its passions."

Grace, mercy, and forgiveness must never be mistaken for tolerance. They are only precursors to the transforming work of the True One. He not only forgives, but He makes people better.

Infinitely better. The hope of the world does not lie in forgiveness alone, for that would be partial. God is far too comprehensive for that. The hope of the world lies in making wrong "livers" right - stronger, more faithful people who peculiarly live out the truth of God, even in difficult times. I suppose the apostle would say it this way: "For the grace of God that brings salvation has appeared to everyone . . . that Christ might redeem us from all iniquity, and purify unto himself a peculiar people, zealous of good works." (Titus 2:14) In Jeremiah, Chapter 23, the prophet spoke about a priesthood that was such a part of their own backslidden culture, they were no longer capable of carrying the Word of God to His people. God said that both prophet and priest spoke their own words to the people, not God's words. It finally became so problematic that God said, through His prophet, He would have to raise up a new generation of shepherds who will not destroy His sheep.

Dr. Martin Case is that kind of shepherd. I mean the kind that looks and acts and speaks like the Good Shepherd. He is a trusted and beloved colleague and friend. He refuses to go along with a culture on the broad path, not because he is contumacious, but because it is worth whatever risks exist to be a part of God's plan for saving us from ourselves. Although it flies in the face of our culture to say, "Thou shall not," Dr. Case believes more in the God over culture than the religious tone under the culture. I, for one, am profoundly grateful for that. What we have in the ensuing pages is a work born in the heart of a man, a good shepherd, who still believes that salvation is only possible, individually or corporately, when God's voice is heard above the politic of the day. Dr. Case has chosen the path, "Lord, to whom else can we go? Only You have words of eternal life." Read this text carefully. Aspire to do all that the Lord has spoken. And join with me, as together we anticipate the voice of the Divine saying to us one day, "You have been made clean through the words I have spoken to you."

— by President Ron Smith,
Wesley Biblical Seminary
Jackson, Mississippi

The Ten Commandments

And God spoke all these words, saying:

"I am the LORD your God, who brought you out of the land of Egypt, out of the house of bondage.

You shall have no other gods before Me.

You shall not make for yourself a carved image, or any likeness of anything that is in heaven above, or that is in the earth beneath, or that is in the water under the earth; you shall not bow down to them nor serve them. For I, the LORD your God, am a jealous God, visiting the iniquity of the fathers on the children to the third and fourth generations of those who hate Me, but showing mercy to thousands, to those who love Me and keep My commandments.

You shall not take the name of the LORD your God in vain, for the LORD will not hold him guiltless who takes His name in vain.

Remember the Sabbath day, to keep it holy. Six days you shall labor and do all your work, but the seventh day is the Sabbath of the LORD your God. In it you shall do no work: you, nor your son, nor your daughter, nor your male servant, nor your female servant, nor your cattle, nor your stranger who is within your gates. For in six days the LORD made the heavens and the earth, the sea, and all that is in them, and rested the seventh day. Therefore the LORD blessed the Sabbath day and hallowed it.

Honor your father and your mother, that your days may be long upon the land which the LORD your God is giving you.

You shall not murder.

You shall not commit adultery.

You shall not steal.

You shall not bear false witness against your neighbor.

You shall not covet your neighbor's house; you shall not covet your neighbor's wife, nor his male servant, nor his female servant, nor his ox, nor his donkey, nor anything that is your neighbor's" (Exodus 20:1-17).

THE TEN COMMANDMENTS: An Introduction

Many people in the secular media along with, unfortunately, some from our own religious organizations,
have tried to convince us that the Ten Commandments were
designed for the ancient world of ages past. They explain that
these laws no longer mesh with the advanced thinking of a
modern world. A recent attempt by a civil liberties group to have
the Ten Commandments removed from a courtroom wall in
Alabama received wide-spread publicity. However, the local
judge in whose court room they hung stood his ground, bravely
challenging the efforts to remove them.

Along with prayer and Bible reading, the Ten Commandments
have been pushed aside in our public schools. No longer are they
taught as the foundation for moral choices or as the bedrock of
our legal system. A September, 1998 *Reader's Digest* article quoted
Ted Turner, the ultra-wealthy television magnate, about his religious views. He said bluntly, "Christianity is a religion for losers."
Then, concerning the Ten Commandments, he added his opinion
saying that some of them were simply "obsolete." He revealed
that he had actually written his own version in 1979 and carries a

copy of this in his wallet. He amended the first one to read, "Love and respect the planet Earth and all living things thereon, especially my fellow species, mankind." The third one read, "Promise to have no more than two children or no more than my nation suggests." Since then he amended that to read "one child." His tenth commandment pledges loyalty, not to a god or government but to "the United Nations and its efforts to collectively improve the conditions of the planet."

We could gather many more examples like this of how the Ten Commandments have been pushed aside and branded "obsolete," but the real need is to identify why such widespread disregard and misunderstanding ever occurred. The root cause of this seems to be ignorance of the original purpose and intent of these inspired words from God.

Contrary to popular belief, the Ten Commandments were not given to make human beings miserable!

C.S. Lewis, a British theologian and author, wrote about a school boy being asked, "What do you think God is like?" He answered, "The best I can determine is that He's someone who snoops around to see if anyone is having fun, and if they are, He puts a stop to it!" How far that is from the truth we have in Scripture!

The truth about the Ten Commandments is that they are a gift from a loving God. They were given by Him who gave life so that life would work the way it was meant to work. Think about it. Who should know best about how something should operate if not the maker of it? In regard to trying to operate any complicated device it has often been said, "When in doubt, read the directions." In a real sense then the Ten Commandments are like a manufacturer's handbook and have been given to us by our Creator to help us get the most out of what He has made. The Ten Commandments, when carefully studied and obeyed, should make our lives run more smoothly. They are the best set of instructions we could receive.

The Psalmist saw this fact clearly. In fact, David saw God's law as a normal and logical extension of the beauty and order he observed in the universe around him. Notice the grand and musical words of Psalm 19 as David moves without a break from praising God's created universe to praising God's Scriptural law:

"The heavens declare the glory of God;
And the firmament shows His handiwork.
Day unto day utters speech,
And night unto night reveals knowledge.
There is no speech nor language
Where their voice is not heard.
Their line has gone out through all the earth,
And their words to the end of the world.
In them He has set a tabernacle for the sun,
Which is like a bridegroom coming out of his chamber,
And rejoices like a strong man to run its race.
Its rising is from one end of heaven,
And its circuit to the other end;
And there is nothing hidden from its heat.
The law of the LORD is perfect, converting the soul;
The testimony of the LORD is sure, making wise the simple;
The statutes of the LORD are right, rejoicing the heart;
The commandment of the LORD is pure, enlightening the eyes;
The fear of the LORD is clean, enduring forever;*

The judgments of the LORD are true and righteous altogether.
More to be desired are they than gold,
Yea, than much fine gold;
Sweeter also than honey and the honeycomb.
Moreover by them Your servant is warned,
And in keeping them there is great reward....

When that psalm is read and studied, one can feel the strong emphasis David has placed on the greatness of God's written law. He is actually more powerful in his praise and description of that than he is of the splendor of the sun and stars.

To David, the wonder and beauty of creation was only surpassed by the wonder and beauty of God's Word. In Psalm 119, with its 176 verses making it the longest chapter in the Bible, David extended his praise of God's law by devoting almost every verse to some good characteristic or use of God's commandments. In verse 62, he actually seems to be getting carried away: "At midnight I rise to praise you, because of your righteous ordinances." Can you imagine getting up at midnight to praise God for the Ten Commandments? If word of such behavior became public, one would quickly be branded "strange" at the very least! After all, is the law not constantly putting up a stop sign to restrict our lives? Is it not constantly whistling a "foul," sounding a siren, or flashing a light to stop our progress? We read David's psalm and ask, "How could anyone sing praises for the law, much less equate it with the wonders of creation?"

Here is how that could happen. Over his lifetime, David, again and again, discovered that God's laws made his life better. He said in Psalm 19:8 that the law causes a person to be happy. What he meant was that without the law there is confusion. Without the law things are constantly thrown into chaos, but where the law is in force and when God's law is obeyed, life works best!

There were many in David's day, as in ours, who must have

4

thought the laws David loved were no more than a collection of strange prohibitions whose purpose was to take all the fun out of life. But the Psalmist viewed them as a "light upon his pathway," the source of help and safety as he walked daily in a dangerous world (Psalm 119: 105). Other Bible writers besides David realized that the law was based on God's love. They saw that it was given to man, not to frustrate him, but to bless him.

> **They saw that the fences erected by God's laws were not to keep them out of the fields of pleasure, but to protect those fields of pleasure, preventing the weeds of pain and destruction from getting in to spoil them.**

In Hank Tate's *Discipline—You Can't Succeed Without It!* the following observation was made about literal fences:

Child psychologists discovered an interesting truth several years ago. Contemporary thought assumed that fences on playgrounds made the children feel restricted in their recreation. A consensus was then reached to remove the fences so children would not feel confined. The opposite effect occurred. Researchers found that the children became more inhibited with their activities. They tended to huddle toward the middle of the playground and exhibited signs of insecurity. When the fences were replaced, the children played with greater enthusiasm and freedom. We all need boundaries—something to define the limits of safety and security. Existential thought suggests that boundaries restrict creativity, but as the children on the playground demonstrated, we need a clear understanding of what is safe and acceptable so our creativity can flourish.

Jesus affirmed the need for God's law when He announced His intentions in Matthew 5:17: "*Do not think that I came to destroy the Law or the Prophets. I did not come to destroy but to fulfill...*." Jesus fulfilled the law by keeping it perfectly. He revealed the fullness that obedience to God's law can bring to a life. He went beyond keeping the law with only an outward obedience—as in obeying a stop sign—and revealed the inward power God can give it to change even the desire of a person's heart and the attitude of a person's mind.

The Apostle Paul had much to say about the law, too. He noted that it was impossible for any human being to keep every demand of the law. However, he said that failure on our part was actually good because it revealed our weaknesses and shortcomings. The law is God's standard. As we fall very short of it, we realize our need for His power and grace. The prophet Amos saw the law as God's plumb-line, making evident our crookedness. The perfection of the law makes clear our need for a Savior. When we accept Christ as our Savior, acknowledging our crookedness and weakness, He gives us Himself—in the form of His Holy Spirit—and then He in us, meets the requirements of God's law. "*For what the law could not do in that it was weak through the flesh, God did by sending His own Son in the likeness of sinful flesh, on account of sin: He condemned sin in the flesh, that the righteous requirement of the law might be fulfilled in us who do not walk according to the flesh but according to the Spirit*" (Romans 8:3,4).

Instead of being a condemning negative, God's law or divine standard is then a life-giving positive which enables us to get the help we need to make our lives the best they can be. Think about a coach who commands his team to run three miles every day, lift weights five days a week, be in bed by eleven o'clock, never smoke, drink, or do drugs, attend every class, and watch the weekly game films. The team would most likely grumble and complain at so many restrictions on their "freedom," but how their attitude would change when such restrictions put them into such good shape that they were able to win a championship! When interviewed after such an accomplishment, the team members would certainly give credit to the demanding require- ments of their coach. "He laid down the law to us," they might say. "He made demands that we might end up with victory!"

The attitude that has relegated God's law to a place in the unenlightened past has caused damage to our nation as a whole. The rise in school violence and the tragic repercussions in our communities illustrate this vividly. Some would say that we need to write and enforce new and stronger laws to combat the evils of our society, but I believe that they are wrong.

We do not need new laws; we need to rediscover and obey the original ten God gave us centuries ago.

Look at the headlines of your daily paper. Listen to the evening news. Open your eyes to the pain, confusion, chaos, and lawlessness in your own community, and then ask yourself, " Is our world really better off since we have neglected God's original instructions?"

The hanging of the Ten Commandments in schools and public places would certainly be a step in the right direction for our nation, but the truth is that until the Ten Commandments are brought back into the daily life of God's people, and until parents teach these precious principles to their own children, God's law will never find its way back into the courtrooms, streets, or media of our land. How seriously do you take God's instructions for your life? Isn't it time you took a fresh look at the Ten Commandments?

The First Commandment:

No Other Gods!

When the Ten Commandments were recorded in Exodus 20, they were given by God to Moses for the people of Israel. The First Commandment reads: "*I am the* LORD *your God, who brought you out of the land of Egypt, out of the house of bondage. You shall have no other gods before Me.*" Later, in the book of Deuteronomy, which means the second giving of the Law, Moses reiterated the Ten Commandments and added these strong words in chapter six: "*Hear, O Israel: The* LORD *our God, the* LORD *is one! You shall love the* LORD *your God with all your heart, with all your soul, and with all your strength. And these words which I command you today shall be in your heart. You shall teach them diligently to your children, and shall talk of them when you sit in your house, when you walk by the way, when you lie down, and when you rise up*"(Deuteronomy 6:4-8).

Put God first!——that is the essence of the First Commandment. The biggest problem most of us have in life today relates to the proper setting of priorities. We fail to put first things first. In some areas of life we do all right. We make our lists of things to do, being careful to put the most important at the top, or we stack our bills to be paid in relation to their "urgency." In many ways every day we are "priority-driven"—constantly trying to decide which things ought to be first.

> **Yet, in our spiritual development, we fail to do things in the order of their importance, and that neglect puts everything else we do on a shaky foundation.**

George Buttrick, a renowned preacher of another day, came upon a farmer who had just retrieved a lost sheep. When Buttrick asked how sheep manage to wander away, the farmer replied, "They just nibble themselves lost. They go," he explained, "from one clump of grass to another until at last they have lost their way."[1] That is the danger we face—nibbling our way from one activity to another until life is gone, and we are left wondering what has happened. Many of us go through the duties of everyday life as if we were on "automatic pilot" with no real consciousness of the overall purpose of our lives or any sense of what is really important.

The First Commandment stops that nibbling-through-life attitude by calling us to establish a main focus for our lives—a relationship with God. Review its wording: *"You shall have no other gods before Me."* If God put this first, it must be very important. There are three questions that we can try to answer to help us get at just how important it is to give God the top spot in our lives. The first one is this: **Who is this God who gives the Ten Commandments?**

The Author of the Ten Commandments is the God of history. In the introduction to the Ten Commandments in Deuteronomy 20, verse 1, God spoke these words, "I am the LORD *your God, who brought you out of the land of Egypt, out of the house of slavery....*" He had already revealed Himself to Abraham, and because of Abraham's faith, He had promised to make him the father of a great nation (Genesis 17:1,2). He had revealed Himself to Abraham's son Isaac: "*And the* LORD *appeared to him the same night and said, 'I am the God of your father Abraham; do not fear, for I am with you. I will bless you and multiply your descendants for My servant Abraham's sake'*" (Genesis 26:24 NKJV). God later revealed Himself to Isaac's son Jacob: "*I am the* LORD *God of Abraham your father and the God of Isaac; the land on which you lie I will give to you and your descendants. Also your descendants shall be as the dust of the earth; you shall spread abroad to the west and the east, to the north and the south; and in you and in your seed all the families of the earth shall be blessed.*" (Genesis 28:13-14 NKJV). This same God was with Joseph who was sold into Egypt by his jealous brothers, the sons of Jacob. This was the God who multiplied the family of Jacob in Egypt. This was the God who saw their bondage to Pharaoh and brought a child named Moses from an Israelite home to live in the palace and grow up to become the deliverer of Israel from out of that slavery.

So, who is the God of the Ten Commandments? He is the God of our history. He is the One about whom the Old Testament keeps a record. He has continually used His power and wisdom on behalf of His people from generation to generation. He has a record that can be trusted.

Yet, He is more than the God of history. **He is also the God of creation.** Prior to the giving of the Ten Commandments, God instructed Moses to prepare to receive these laws. Exodus 19: 3-5 records the words of that meeting: "*And Moses went up to God, and the* LORD *called to him from the mountain, saying, 'Thus you shall say to the house of Jacob, and tell the children of Israel: "You have seen what I did to the Egyptians, and how I bore you on eagles' wings and brought you to Myself. Now therefore, if you will indeed obey My voice and keep My covenant, then you shall be a special treasure to Me above all people; for all the earth is Mine."'*" What a statement: "*all the earth is Mine*"! The whole earth is His because God created all things. He is the sovereign, eternal Creator! And He laid down the laws that make life work.

Not only is He the God of history and creation, **our God is the God of covenant.** In Exodus 19:5 God told Moses, "Now *therefore, if you will indeed obey My voice and keep My covenant, then you shall be a special treasure to Me above all people...."*

The covenant to which God was referring was the Ten Commandments. These ten statements are an expression of the character of our great God. In them we see how God thinks and what God desires for His people. If the people would keep the covenant, they were promised God's blessings. As the God of history, of creation, and of covenant, He had and still has every right to command, *"You shall have no other gods before Me."* This brings us to the second question, **"What did this God really want?"** The overall answer is this: God wanted to be God alone within the lives of all people in all the world in all times. If this is so, you might wonder, why didn't He create human beings so that they would automatically worship and serve Him? The answer is simple. Such creatures could not show genuine love. There can be no genuine love unless there exists the capacity to choose, to make a decision, to accept or reject love. So, God created people with the capacity to choose. They could love Him or not love Him. This was risky because some would never choose Him, but God was willing to take the risk for those who would.

God wanted His called-out people to worship and serve Him, not because He needed anything from anyone, but because in so doing, they would be establishing their lives on the right foundation. If that priority were rightly set, the other things in their lives would most certainly line up correctly. After all, He is the only right and true God that there is to worship. There is no superior power to the One who created everything! He longed to bless and teach His covenant people in the way that they should go so that they could live full, rich, and meaningful lives. He also wanted to use them to be His witnesses to the world, telling everyone of His holiness, power, and great love. This is why God began as He did with the Ten Commandments. Unless people acknowledge and worship Him as the only true God, nothing else they do will be of any lasting value to them or Him. Some call this "vest-button" theology. If you don't get that first button right, none of the rest will ever line up!

Some critics have said that the language of the First Commandment is archaic. They suppose that having "other gods" is not truly a modern problem because we do not consciously observe polytheism, the belief in many gods. Many think the more current problem to be addressed is the lack of acknowledgement of any god at all. These would edit the commandment to read: *"You shall have at least one god."* But God knew what He was doing. He knew that He had created human beings with a void that only He could fill. He knew that without His direction and intervention they would foolishly look in many places for something to fill their emptiness, remaining ignorant of the fact that only the God of history, creation, and covenant could bring the fullness for which they longed. The danger is not that modern man will recognize no god at all; the danger is that other so-called gods of our own invention will be given priority in our lives—ahead of or instead of the one true God revealed in the Bible.

When first place is given to anything or anyone instead of God, our lives rest on uncertain footing, and we are left vulnerable to deception, misdirection, and emptiness.

Dr. Paul Rees told about a couple who worshipped and served God early in their married life. However, as they moved off to the big city and became more prosperous, they forgot God. Years passed and they lost contact with the village of their youth. On a trip that took them near it, they decided to drive through that village. As they topped the hill and saw the village ahead, the man said, "Well, dear, that's where we started out." With a sigh that revealed an emptiness within, the wife replied, "And sometimes I wonder where we've gotten to!"

Augustine's quote about God filling the spiritual void in us is repeated again and again. Remembering the emptiness of his life in those days when he was driven by selfish passion he said, "Thou hast made us for Thyself, and our hearts are restless until they find their rest in Thee." We can only be "whole"—with all the empty places filled—when He is our God and our only God.

One final question will help us further understand the importance of the First Commandment. It is this: **How do we let God be the only god in our lives?** First, we must acknowledge that *"there is one God the Father"* (1 Corinthians. 8:5,6). This is God, the Creator of all things, the God of Abraham, Isaac, and Jacob, the God of the Old Testament, and the God and Father of Jesus Christ. The Bible testifies over and over about the truth of His power and character, and so we have a solid basis for recognizing His existence. Secondly, we must acknowledge that *"from Him are all things."* Everything we have comes from this God: life, strength, blessings, earth's beauties—everything! The epistle of James reminds us that *"every good and perfect gift is from above and comes down from the Father of lights, with whom there is no variation or shadow of turning"*(James 1:17). In Acts, Paul urged his Athenian audience not only to recognize that all material things come from God but also every man's human life as well: *"And He has made from one blood every nation of men to dwell on all the face of the earth, and has determined their preappointed times and the boundaries of their dwellings, so that they should* seek the Lord, in the hope that they might grope for Him and find Him, though He is not far from each one of us; for in Him we live and move and have our being . . ." (Acts 17:26-28). God created us to be His own, to return His love, to praise Him, to serve Him in the world, and to live with Him forever.

So, after this is accepted and believed, how do we approach so wonderful a God? He has provided the way to Himself through Jesus Christ; "I am the way, the truth, and the life. No one comes to the Father except through Me" (John 14:6).

In the Old Testament people were commanded to keep the Ten Commandments and receive God's blessings or fail to keep them and receive His curses. However, God knew even then that they would often fail, and so He mercifully provided a system of sacrifice whereby they could confess their sins and receive forgiveness. These animal sacrifices pointed toward the One perfect sacrifice that Jesus would offer for the sins of the whole world.

Today, through faith in Jesus, we have part of an even better covenant than the old one that depended on obedience to the Ten Commandments. Jesus spoke of this at the Last Supper, "Drink from this, all of you, for this is my blood of the new covenant, which is poured out for many for the forgiveness of sins" (Matthew 26:27,28).

We could not reach God by ourselves, so Jesus brought God to us.

Through faith in Him, He can be established in our lives as the one true God, and He will empower us to "have no other gods before Him."

All of the Ten Commandments are still true and valuable.

However, unless God is your God, unless He is first in all things, you will never have the power to obey them and find out just how appropriate His commandments are for establishing the rest of life's priorities in a way that pleases God and brings you peace and joy. "*I am the* LORD *your God...you shall have no other gods before Me.*" If you are longing for a life that has real meaning and purpose, examine your priorities. You must put God first.

A Scottish newspaper ran a religious ad on the front page. Inside a box in a very visible spot were some words written in bold print: **"Look at the back page!"** The back page was blank, except in very small print in the right corner were these words: **"Is this where you are putting God?"** If our answer to that question happens to be "yes," then the chances are good that "other gods" will take over the "front page" of our lives. Giving the Creator God His rightful place is the only way to win out over false gods and really begin to experience the fullness of life.

The Second Commandment:

No Idols!

Exodus 20:1-6: *Then God spoke all these words: I am the Lord your God, who brought you out of the land of Egypt, out of the house of slavery; you shall have no other gods before me. You shall not make for yourself an idol, whether in the form of anything that is in heaven above, or that is on the earth beneath, or that is in the water under the earth. You shall not bow down to them or worship them; for I the Lord your God am a jealous God, punishing children for the iniquity of parents, to the third and the fourth generation of those who reject me, but showing steadfast love to the thousandth generation of those who love me and keep my commandments.*

In the previous chapter it was shown that the Ten Commandments describe the moral foundation laid down by God for human life. We saw that the Ten Commandments were never meant to fence us in. Instead they were to set us free to fulfill and enjoy God's great design for life on this planet. Of course, He as the Creator and Grand Designer knows the best way for us to live in His world. So each commandment is like a loving, thoughtful gift to be used in making the road of life smoother and our whole journey more satisfying. Just following the first one, allowing only God on the throne of our hearts, would eliminate the frequently wrong choices we make when we allow self or Satan to usurp that control. God made us for Himself and for Himself alone. Only He can satisfy the deepest desires of our lives.

The Second Commandment is just as vital as the first. It is the longest of all the commandments, but begins with a short and simple statement, *"You shall not make for yourself an idol,"* or as the King James Version has it, *"any graven image."* At first reading, there are probably none of us who are really worried about breaking this Second Commandment. We are rather like the man who, after hearing his pastor preach long and persuasively about the danger of breaking any of the Ten Commandments, remarked, "Well, at least I never made any graven images!"[2] We think of ourselves as far removed from the Hittites, Jebusites, and even sometimes the Israelites who struggled with idol-worship. We feel no connection to such backward and obviously heathen practices. However, we might be surprised to read that the greatest punishment described for breaking any of the commandments is reserved for this second one. Evidently, God considers it to be a very serious matter. Notice verses five and six: *"You shall not bow down to them or worship them; for I the* LORD *your God am a jealous God, punishing children for the iniquity of parents, to the third and the fourth generation of those who reject me . . ."*

What a severe penalty was promised to idolaters! Their families would feel the consequences for three or four generations. Yet many of us have difficulty thinking that we in this modern age are really at risk of causing such long-term trouble for our families. Perhaps this commandment applied to the ancient world where there were idols everywhere but could not really have an application to our lives today. However, like it or not, the commandment is there, and really should be examined carefully. I believe that if we look at it seriously, we will find, as with the First Commandment, that it, too, is a special gift and significant key designed by God to help us in our daily lives. It is not meant to put us down or to make life difficult, but rather to expand the horizons of our lives. Obedience to it will not make our lives smaller and less beautiful, but fuller, more beautiful, and far more satisfying.

God chose to place this commandment in the number two spot. He obviously is quite serious about its importance in all our lives. In the days when the Scriptures were still being written, this command prohibiting idol worship was emphasized often by the pious Jews and their fiery prophets. They recognized that most of the times that Israel strayed away from God, idolatry—the worship of some kind of idol—was the sin that led them away. For example, when Moses was on Mount Sinai receiving the Ten Commandments from God, the people were down in the valley melting their jewelry to make an image of a calf. And, as Moses appeared with the tablets to present them to the people as God's word for them, they were bowing down and dancing around that golden calf.

> **They wanted to worship
> something they could see.
> They wanted a god on whom
> they could keep an eye!**

Later, their own prophets preached to them that such idol worship was not only sickening but absurd. We still admire those great prophets for their vision of the coming Messiah and their perceptive social consciousness, but there was nothing that they addressed that caused them to speak with more passion than the issue of idol worship. Listen to Jeremiah in chapter ten of his prophecy: *"For the customs of the peoples are worthless; they cut a tree out of the forest, and a craftsman shapes it with his chisel. They adorn it with silver and gold; they fasten it with hammer and nails so it will not totter. Like a scarecrow in a melon patch, their idols cannot speak; they must be carried because they cannot walk. Do not fear them; they can do no harm nor can they do any good"* (Jeremiah 10:3-5).

As many of the prophets had done before and after him, Jeremiah was explaining that idol worship was completely illogical. It is absurd to give any attention to an idol—especially one that has been made by the one who worships it! There are many more references that could be given from Jeremiah and the other prophets which describe the foolishness of idol worship. We could all agree with them and simply stop our study, discard this commandment as not necessary for our lives, and move to the next one. However, God makes no mistakes and wastes no words. If He included this commandment among His short list of ten, we must take time to dig a little deeper until we find out just how it applies to our lives right now.

Where is the harm in worshipping idols? The danger of idolatry is simply this: anything that gets more of our attention, interest, or devotion than God gets causes our value-system and our very lives to get dangerously off track. Idol-worship encourages a false perception of God. It blurs a person's vision of who He really is, and God hates anything that blurs His image. Actually, it all goes back to the First Commandment. There God made clear that He wants to be our only God. We are to allow no others to compete with our love for Him. Think of this: God on His throne, being worshipped by His people. How we perceive God affects everything else in our lives, and that is why God is against anything that blurs or distorts a proper perception of Him.

Such distortion falls into two specific categories. First, since an idol is something that can be seen, it limits the reality of who God really is. Israel appreciated the supernatural help of Jehovah God who was constantly intervening for them, but they were distressed that they could not see Him. They longed for a god they could see. In a sense, we all do. One little boy once tried to solve this. He was busily drawing a picture and his mother asked, "What are you drawing?" Without stopping, he replied, "I am drawing a picture of God." She said, "But no one knows what God looks like." He looked up at her proudly and said, "They will when I get through!"[3]

People like to have something they can see. Idol worshipers want a visible god, a god they can see—a god they can comprehend. However, would we really and truly want to serve a god that we could fully comprehend? Would we want a God that our limited faculties could completely understand? Such a god would not really be much of a god; he would be too close to our ordinary level of life. But that is exactly what so many people want—a god who can be seen and comprehended and, consequently, a god who can be manipulated and controlled for their own purposes.

That introduces the second attraction of idol worship.

An idol is not only visible, but it is also seemingly safe. An idol that can be seen and understood is not going to make any demands.

An idol cannot speak, as Jeremiah's words made clear earlier. It is manageable. It is predictable. C. S. Lewis wrote a series of books called the *Chronicles of Narnia*. Narnia was an imaginary land whose inhabitants symbolized different things in the spiritual world. In the volume called *The Lion, the Witch, and the Wardrobe*, Susan and Lucy stepped through the wardrobe or closet into an imaginary land called Narnia. There they met and spoke to the beaver about Aslan the lion. The beaver began to tell them that

Aslan the lion was the king of Narnia. He ruled over everything. He was the great king. Susan responded, "Oh, I thought he was a man. Is he quite safe? I think I would be very anxious if I had to talk to a lion." The beaver answered, "Well, if your knees did not knock you would be more brave than anyone else, or else you are very silly." Lucy spoke up again, "Then he is not safe?" Mr. Beaver replied, "Who said anything about being safe? Of course he is not safe. But he is good." That is precisely the way it is when you follow Jesus Christ. He is not always safe. I find that to be true. Sometimes He disturbs my plans. He rearranges my priorities. He bothers my conscience, but He is good. He is holy. He is righteous, and everything He does for me is always for the best. But that is not the way it is with idols. Idols can be manipulated, moved, and changed because they cannot respond. They are safe.

So far, we have still not specifically seen what idol worship has to do with us. Do idols still show up in our modern, enlightened world? Well, in what many scholars believe was the last book written for the New Testament, the epistle of First John, we can read that apostle's very last warning to Christians: "*Little children, keep yourselves from idols*" (1 John 5:21). He was very aware that idolatry can be a problem even in the lives of Christian believers.

The danger of idols in our day is that they show up in disguise. We do not immediately recognize them as idols.

They are things that subtly move into our lives to become substitutions for the true God. They consume our interest; they dominate our conversation; they even move us to release large amounts of our income. The commandment makes clear what God thinks of this: *"Do not make to yourself any idol, for I am a jealous God."*

Have you ever been jealous? God feels a righteous jealousy. He made you for Himself and when something hurts that relationship, God is jealous. God cannot and will not stand for any competition for His position as LORD of All. God is hurt by our substitutions. He is offended. Anything that draws our affection from Him, He opposes. But offending God is not the only damage caused by idolatry. The Second Commandment assures us that our actions will affect our children, grandchildren, and even great-grand children. Think about it. When God is established as supreme in a home, when He is the focus and flavor of our conversation, thinking, and actions, our children see and are drawn to the truth and security He provides. They in turn will live that way before their children, and most likely those children will live that example before theirs. However, false worship or idolatry, a consuming interest in the things of this world, will also be passed on for generations. Examine your own family tree. What is the most important connection between generations? Is it beautiful possessions, advanced academic accomplishments, expertise in sports, or social service? Or, do you share above all a love for God? We must become aware of the importance of obeying this commandment against idolatry. Damage caused by ignoring it can spill over to hurt several generations.

While there are thousands of illustrations of idolatry in America that could be cited here, we will examine only four broad categories into which most of them seem to fall. **First of all, there is the idolatry of things.** We live in a material culture. We like our "stuff." Of course, we do have to have many things to function normally. We need such things as food, shelter, clothing, and transportation. In fact, Paul even told Timothy that God *"has provided for us all things, richly to enjoy"* (1 Timothy 6:17) but warned that no one is to trust in *"uncertain riches but in the living God"* who gave them.

We must heed this warning because even important and essential things can slip into such a high place in our lives that they become idols, demanding time and attention as if they had the same right to command us as our LORD God has. There is a very simple barrier we can erect to keep this kind of idolatry out of our lives; it is called gratitude. When we consciously and constantly give thanks to God for the material things He has let us use, we will be more consistently focused on Him as our true Provider. Without Him, we would have nothing. He owns it all! So, thank God freely for your "stuff." Practice this frequently. You can say, "Thank you, God, for this boat" or "these golf clubs which You have allowed me to enjoy." Take nothing for granted. Only as you consistently see the material things in your life as gifts from God can you really keep them in their proper place.

The second big category of idolatry in our modern day is sex. Now be sure of this: God is for sex. He invented it. It was His great idea! It was part of His plan for us. When sex is used according to God's plan, it not only brings pleasure to the man and wife, it glorifies God. That is why He gave the laws to protect the sacredness of sex. God, in essence, put a fence around sex and said, "This is something that I do not want to see abused. Do not make it common, earthly, or dirty. It is beautiful." But do you see what America has done? Is it wrong to conclude that America has turned sex into an idol? Just look at the television programming. Look at the news-stands. Look anywhere at all. Just look! Radio, television, advertising, and music bombard the world with sex. We as Americans have certainly made sex an idol. It controls our thinking. It influences our buying. It sets the standard for beauty and popularity. It consumes us and dares to take the place of God.

On my regular walk through the University of Mississippi

campus, I often pick up a copy of the college newspaper. Imagine my surprise when I read a story reprinted in *The Daily Mississippian* from a North Dakota student named Sherri Richards who agreed with my assessment about the idolatry of sex. In commenting on a new "reality" series which featured four unmarried but committed couples exposed to the temptations put forth by twenty-six "sexy singles," Ms. Richards was not amused at the showcasing of "carnal instincts and hormonal urges." She went on to explain:

> And, in the process, [they] defy all moral principles that any decent human being has . . . Who does this? Who goes on an island to try to tempt someone in a committed relationship? Sick, sick people, that's who . . . Who would go somewhere to be tempted when they're in a committed relationship? . . . It's *Indecent Proposal* all over again. "Honey, go make out with that chick and I'll go hang all over that muscular guy over there, and then we'll be rich! I love you so much!" . . . So who is to blame for this mess? The singles, the couples, FOX [network]? Or maybe it's those who enthusiastically tuned in Wednesday night to watch this brothel. Those people who watched to see relationships destroyed and singles sell themselves for the American dream. But, I guess who can blame them? This is America, the land of the sexed. And it's all too tempting.[4]

Fitting right in with our list of common idols, right after materialism and sex, is the modern-day idol of pleasure. We have heard that all work and no play makes Jack a dull boy, or, in more modern terms, all work and no play fills Jack's life with stress. There is an element of truth in that. God is on the side of balanced living—of rest and revitalization of our bodies. God is glorified when we are able to serve Him and others with minds and bodies that are rested and healthy. However, is it not obvious that we have come too much to idolize leisure and pleasure? We take that which is good and allow it to become an idol. We lose the proper balance of work and rest. We begin to demand our right to leisure and give too much attention to the pursuit of entertainment. We selfishly guard "our own time" and begin to neglect and even despise *"the good works He has prepared for us to walk in"* (Ephesians 2:10).

The idolatry of leisure and pleasure deadens us to the voice of God, and we fail to do the things that would please Him, thereby missing the very things that would bring eternal joy and rest to our lives.

One example of the enormous influence that our preoccupation with leisure and recreation has produced can be seen in our passion for sports. Take football, for example.

In the South, where I live, that sport has taken on many of the trappings of religion. People find their "connectedness" over long spans of time, even generations, through shared enthusiasm for a certain college team. Men and women who would be unlikely models for Christian T-shirts and certainly unwilling to apply Christian bumper stickers, will proudly wear team colors, even outrageous costumes complete with body-paint, decorate their vehicles, spend thousands of dollars, and travel hundreds of miles to watch the performance of their beloved team.

Some of our stadiums would rival the ancient temple architecture of the Greeks and Romans, and the sport even has its own liturgy of cheers, chants, and music.

At least the painter of one sports banner which appeared in 1996 at Lambeau Field when the Green Bay Packers were Super Bowl bound recognized the sport for what it has really become to many—idolatry. Read the following and see if you agree with such a categorization.

Our Favre, who art in Lambeau, hallowed be thy arm. The Bowl will come, it will be won, in New Orleans as it is in Lambeau. Give us this Sunday our weekly win. And give us many touchdown passes. But do not let others pass against us. Lead us not into frustration, but deliver us to Bourbon Street. For thine is the MVP, the best of the NFL, and the glory of the cheeseheads, now and forever. Go get 'em![5]

Former University of Alabama coach Mike Dubose learned the hard way about the danger of putting pleasure before God. In a newspaper interview for the *Dothan Eagle* on November 26, 2000, he told reporter Debbie Ingram Smith about his conversion to Christ after meeting his wife and attending her church. However, Dubose expressed regret about that time in his life: "I made a mistake. I didn't get into the Word. I didn't develop a personal relationship with Him. I got into the flesh. I got into the world and I was enjoying it. I told myself I would live the good life, and when I am an old, old man I will make it right. That's what lots of people do." In 1998 there was public outrage at his extramarital affair with his secretary. This was followed by equally intense criticism of his coaching ability when the Crimson Tide failed to make it to the national championship. It was then that Dubose said he began to ask some tough questions about his personal life and his future. He did some real soul-searching, and those who know him best say he is a changed man. He is on God's team now and even finds the idolatry of football troubling: "When I pull up to the stadium and see those thousands of people there, with such a passion for the game of football, I ask myself, 'Do they have the same passion for God?' For 99 percent of them, I'd say no."

There is another category of idolatry that might surprise some people—the idolatry of religion. Although there are many things that could be said about this category of idolatry, we will examine just two. First our modern culture has developed a fascination with angels. Even my own wife enjoys collecting little angel figurines, and such a thing can be quite innocent. After all, angels are mentioned all through the Bible as being sent by God to do marvelous things for people. However, there seems to be a cult developing among non-Christians throughout the world which elevates angels to the place of gods. Part of the appeal of the non-Biblical television and movie depiction of angels has been explained by modern observers. *Time Magazine* explained the current popularity of angels as due to the fact that they are perceived "as all fluff and meringue, kind, non-judgmental, available to everyone, like aspirin." *Christianity Today* warned, "Angels too easily provide a temptation for those who want a 'fix' of spirituality without bothering with God Himself."[6] However, the Bible teaches that angels only work in our lives as *"ministering spirits"* under the direct authority of God (Hebrews 1:14). They are certainly real and have probably touched the lives of every

Christian, but it is to God alone that all thanks and praise should be given. Jesus Christ is above every angel. There is a danger of worshipping angels instead of the LORD who created and controls them.

Another way that religion becomes an idol is when the church and a person's membership in it is elevated above a relationship with God Himself. The church began with Jesus Christ; it belongs to Him. He called it His Body. Our local group of believers is to be obedient to His direction. Church membership is not an end in itself. It is a means to an end. It is the Body that does whatever Christ the Head directs. Whenever we make our local church independent of the Headship of Jesus, or even separate from other bodies of Christian believers, we have made church our idol. The church is to be about the business of the Heavenly Father. She should be pointing men and women to Jesus Christ, nurturing them in the faith, and providing a channel through which they may serve God and be His people.

The experience of a young woman from Finland who is now in America to head up our church's children's ministry offered this insight. As a small child, the parents of Mona Stenbom took her to the Lutheran Church of Finland, the state church, where she was baptized. The family seldom attended after that until Mona was fifteen. At that age, all the young people attended extended confirmation classes. She participated in that class and the service of confirmation but then rarely returned. Her name was on the membership list, but the church had become like an idol. Membership there seemed to excuse one from a real relationship with Jesus Christ Himself. Later, as a high school senior, she came to America as an exchange student. She lived with a family in Laurel, Mississippi, and there she learned something new about the church. She saw that belonging to a church was not an end in itself but instead was a means of getting to know God and His Word. It was a place used for joining with others in service as

He directed. With the encouragement and direction of that host family and that church, she came to have a personal relationship with Jesus Christ. Because she came to see that the church is not an idol, she is in full-time Christian work today.

> ## The church is a place; the church is His body; and most importantly, the church is any place where His body gathers to worship and serve Him.

Oh, what a difference this truth can make! We must have no idols. God has given us material things, sex, pleasure, and religion to help us and to bless us. Yet, if we let any of the things God has given or made have such a strong hold on us that we neglect to seek Him and His will above all, we have committed idolatry and should not be surprised when severe trouble results. Let this powerful warning from the fortieth chapter of Isaiah summarize the foolishness of idolatry as we close this chapter:

> *To whom then will you liken God? Or what likeness will you compare to Him? The workman molds an image, the goldsmith overspreads it with gold, and the silversmith casts silver chains. Whoever is too impoverished for such a contribution chooses a tree that will not rot; he seeks for himself a skillful workman to prepare a carved image that will not totter. Have you not known? Have you not heard? Has it not been told you from the beginning? Have you not understood from the foundations of the earth? It is He who sits above the circle of the earth, and its inhabitants are like grasshoppers, who stretches out the heavens like a curtain, and spreads them out like a tent to dwell in. He brings the princes to nothing; He makes the judges of the earth useless . . . "To*

whom will you liken Me, or to whom shall I be equal?" says the Holy
One. Lift up your eyes on high, and see who has created these things,
Who brings out their host by number; He calls them all by name, by
the greatness of His might and the strength of His power; not one is
missing.

This is the God who calls us to worship Him, to know Him, to
serve Him, and to be loved by Him. Remove all idols from your
life. Let God have the supreme place in your affections. Ask God
to make you obedient to the Second Commandment. Ask Him to
search your heart for hidden idols. Make these wonderful words
from William Cowper's great hymn "Walking with God" your
prayer now:

The dearest idol I have known,
What e'er that idol be,
Help me to tear it from Thy throne,
And worship only Thee!

The Third Commandment:

Use His Name Reverently!

T he King James Version of the Bible delivers the Ten Commandments in powerful yet familiar language. The third one reads: *"Thou shalt not take the name of the* LORD *thy God in vain for the* LORD *will not hold him guiltless who taketh His name in vain"* (Exodus 20:7). Did you get that phrasing, *"Thou shalt not"* ? In our day we much prefer phrasing like this: "I hope you will consider this"; or, "Let me make a suggestion"; or perhaps, "Now here is something for you to think about." We have a tendency to tiptoe around what we perceive to be a personal matter; however, God does not. *"Thou shalt not."* He gets right to the point. He wastes no words. After all, when the commandments were first given, God was directing them to Israel, His hand-picked people, who also happened to be hard-headed and slow to obey. They were people who constantly vacillated between their loyalty to Him—the true but invisible God—and their desire to have idols which they could actually see. To such people then, and unfortunately to such as we are now, God must be direct. We can learn from this no-nonsense approach. One religious group effectively employed it in regard to their church property. They posted a sign that read: "Absolutely No Parking! This means YOU!" signed "The Sisters of Mercy"! At times direct and forceful language must be used in communicating important truths to others and will not at all contradict the love or grace of God.

Now, why did God make such a strong statement about the use of His name? Certainly fear of losing His authority is far from God's thoughts. He has absolutely no reason to be like some human authority figure who insists, "I want to be addressed with respect! You can call me Mr. Smith, not just Bill!" No, God is not insecure about His position. There has to be more to this commandment than simply an uneasiness about our failing to follow some divine protocol in speaking His name.

The real issue dealt with in the Third Commandment is not the use of God's name, but the misuse of it. To take God's name in vain is to misuse it. The root meaning of "vain" is emptiness, uselessness, or wastefulness. God's name is associated with who He is. It is powerful and effective. Jesus mentioned this in His intercessory prayer in John 17: 6 "*I have made <u>Your name</u> known to those whom You gave me from the world. They were Yours, and You gave them to Me, and they have kept Your word....12 While I was with them, I protected them <u>in Your name</u> that You have given me. I guarded them, and not one of them was lost except the one destined to be lost, so that the Scripture might be fulfilled.*" [Emphasis added.]

Even today, God has graciously allowed us to use His powerful name for our needs. This privilege could be compared to someone's letting us have the authority to sign his checks or use his banking card. With such a privilege comes a responsibility to use the power of that name wisely and honestly. We would not want to betray the trust of a friend or misuse his name—which in this case is directly linked to his resources. And yet we do not exercise the same care with God's name as we would in using the assets of a trusted friend. We misuse His good name in many ways. Let us examine a few of them.

The first vain use of God's name that usually comes to mind is including it when cursing. The linking of God's name with a profane phrase or angry oath is so common in the world around us that most of us are no longer shocked to hear it daily. In fact, some folks curse so often that they are completely unaware of doing it. They seem to be compelled to curse— almost addicted to it. As with other addictions, a compulsion to curse develops progressively. Once a person allows himself to express his negative emotions through profanity, he will find that those same words will come to mind the very next time he is upset or excited. Without a conscious awareness and effort to stop this, he will not only find that profanity becomes his normal way of speaking, but he will have to add more and more to his profane vocabulary to get the same emotional release as he did when cursing was new to his conversation. Adding God's name to his oaths will seem to increase their power. Yet, God's precious name was given to believers to build up and heal, not to tear down and destroy.

It is worth mentioning here that Jesus taught about the real source of our spoken words. He said that a person speaks *"out of the abundance of his heart"* (Matthew 12:34).

> **In other words, if a person's language is profane, so is his heart. Using God's name in profanity, then, shows a real problem in the heart of the speaker, especially if the speaker professes to be a Christian.**

Another dangerous characteristic of cursing other than being progressively addictive, is that it is also dangerously contagious. A small boy used a curse word in front of his mother. "Son," she said, "where did you pick up such a word as that?" He answered, "Mr. Jones, our neighbor, uses that word a lot." Profaning God's name, as in other swearing, is a practice picked up and passed on easily to young people who happen to hear it. To them it seems manly or grown-up and so they eagerly make use of it themselves. In such a way, one person's sin is perpetuated in another.

Although it is not often realized by the one employing it, swearing is a mark of insecurity in the one indulging in its use. As a pastor I have lost count of the number of times that someone has cursed in my presence only to have another who knew me remark, "Didn't you know this is the preacher?" This would be followed by a profuse apology, an embarrassed silence, and finally a complete change of tone or subject in the conversation. Obviously, in such cases, the speaker had been "padding" his speech for entertainment value or effect, not secure enough that his plain and true expressions would make others see him favorably. Coupling God's name with profanity to make one's self appear greater is definitely a vain use of it.

There are other ways that God's name is misused besides in profanity. **Using His name insincerely offends Him.** This was pointed out in Leviticus 19:12: "*And you shall not swear by My name falsely, nor shall you profane the name of your God: I am the* LORD." In Old Testament times, just as in our day, people lied so frequently that just saying something simply and plainly failed to be sufficiently convincing. So, different phrases were routinely added to emphasize truthfulness, the most effective being phrases naming God's attributes or requesting His own witness. During Jesus' earthly ministry the oaths and add-on phrases had multiplied to such a degree that honesty seemed hard to discern. His response to such insincerity was recorded in Matthew 5: 33-37: "*Again you have* *heard that it was said to those of old, 'You shall not swear falsely, but shall perform your oaths to the Lord.' But I say to you, do not swear at all: neither by heaven, for it is God's throne, nor by the earth, for it is His footstool; nor by Jerusalem, for it is the city of the great King. Nor shall you swear by your head, because you cannot make one hair white or black. But let your 'Yes' be 'Yes,' and your 'No,' 'No.' For whatever is more than these is from the evil one."*

Jesus knew that if a person were honest, he would not need to swear by God's name, but if he were dishonest, he might stick in God's name to make his listener think he was sincere.

Dr. Clovis Chappell once had such an experience with a man who had come to him for some help. Dr. Chappell listened to the man's pathetic story and gave the man what he wanted. The poor man was so overjoyed that he said, "I'll do anything you want me to do. I'll wash your car!" Dr. Chappell replied, "Okay, come tomorrow morning and wash my car." "I'll be there," the man said, "I'll certainly be there!" Then Dr. Chappell added, "Good. If you show up, you'll be the first one in my twenty-five years of ministry!" The man responded, "I will be there," and, lifting his right hand to heaven said solemnly, "I hope God will strike me dead if I'm not there in the morning to wash your car!" Dr. Chappell explained, "And evidently that's what happened, for I have never seen him since!"[7] Leave God's name out of your promises. Just tell the truth and keep your word. Anything else dishonors His name and your relationship with Him.

There are times when we are required to swear by God's name when such swearing is quite appropriate. In courtrooms, at the altar at weddings, at baptisms, and even in public praying we are expected to use God's name. As with everything spiritual, God requires that not only just the words be right and reverent, but also that the heart of the person calling on His name be sincere in its request or vow. How sincere were you at such times? *"Thou shalt not take the name of the* LORD *thy God in vain"* still holds a mighty warning for us today.

In addition to profanity and insincerity, **there is a danger of being too casual in the use of God's name.** We can become so familiar with God's name that it becomes merely ordinary. The devout ancient Jews feared this possibility. They revered the name of God, *Yahweh*, so much that they would not speak that sacred name out loud except in the temple on the annual Day of Atonement. Why? Because God's name is the very essence of His person. To use that name casually, they believed, was to treat God with contempt. It is no wonder that when the disciples asked Jesus to teach them to pray that He began with the name for God and described the right attitude toward that name: *"Our Father, who art in heaven, hallowed be your name"* (Matthew 6:9). This is the positive statement of the Third Commandment: we are to hallow or see as holy the name of God. Be very careful when you mention God's name that your intentions are sincere and your motives are pure.

Jesus even went a step further in the matter of prayer. He said that we should pray to our Father, being careful to keep His name hallowed or holy, while asking in Jesus' name for what we needed (John 16:23-24). He and the Father are one, but Jesus said we could use His name in prayer, allowing us to sense the closeness a relationship with Him provides. When we use Jesus' name, we must be in a spirit consistent with all that Jesus is and hold faithfully to all that He has taught us about what pleases God.

The disciples learned about the power of Jesus' name. At Pentecost, when the assembled crowd, in awe and fear, asked

Peter what to do, he told them to repent and be baptized *"in the name of Jesus"* (Acts 2:38). When Peter and John came upon a lame man at the temple gate, they commanded him to rise and be healed *"in the name of Jesus"* (Acts 3:6). Later, when authorities asked, *"By what power or by what name did you do this?"* Peter answered that Jesus' name was the only name *"under heaven"* by which a person could be saved (Acts 4:7,12). Paul knew first hand the power of Jesus' name and wrote about it in Philippians 2:9-11. Many believe this to be one of the earliest Christian hymns: *"God also has highly exalted Him and given Him the name which is above every name, that at the name of Jesus every knee should bow, of those in heaven, and of those on earth, and of those under the earth, and that every tongue should confess that Jesus Christ is Lord, to the glory of God."*

The early Christians were convinced about the trustworthiness of the name of Jesus. They sang about His name. They praised His name. They risked everything for His name. The tragedy is that we seem to have lost the sense of glory associated with the name of God and our Savior Jesus Christ. We stumble along when we could be living victoriously through the power of God! We too often hear the *"thou shalt not"* and neglect the implied right we have to draw on His rich resources. We are privileged, encouraged, and even commanded to use His name for our needs and His works, but we are warned to use it carefully, sincerely, lovingly, and faithfully.

The power of a name is awesome! An explorer discovers a new territory and plants a flag in the name of his king or queen. A company is sold after years of carefully maintaining its good name and can demand a high price if the new owners wish to continue operating under that established name. Even families feel the advantage of keeping a good name. Opportunities open up, friendships begin easily, and opinions are quickly accepted if a person has a good family name. How much more powerful, though is Christ's good name? And how much more care should we employ in using it? We Christians should carry carefully the powerful name of our Lord. We should be known by our confident yet always appropriate use of His name. After all, through the mighty name of Jesus we can be forgiven, made heirs of eternal life, and ask amazing things from God in faith. No wonder God commands that His holy, sacred, powerful Name be hallowed and never misused!

Charles Wesley declares the matchless worth of God's name in this great hymn from the United Methodist Hymnal:

O for a thousand tongues to sing
My great Redeemer's praise,
The glories of my God and King,
The triumphs of His grace.

Jesus the name that charms our fears,
That bids our sorrows cease,
'Tis music in the sinner's ears,
'Tis life and health and peace.

My gracious Master and my God,
Assist me to proclaim,
To spread thro' all the earth abroad,
The honors of Thy name.

Yet long before Charles Wesley, the Psalmist, awed by the greatness of the Lord's name, proclaimed, "O *magnify the* LORD *with me, and let us exalt His name together*" (Psalm 34:3). We would do well to obey this request right now.

The Fourth Commandment:

Remember the Sabbath!

S o far, to make the Ten Commandments speak to us in our modern times, we have had to discover not only what the original intent was when they were first given but also how they were restated and reinterpreted in the New Testament in light of the gospel of Jesus Christ. The Fourth Commandment will cause much confusion unless this same plan is followed. So, we will look at it first in its ancient setting.

Surprisingly, this commandment is one of the longest ones: "*Remember the Sabbath day, to keep it holy. Six days you shall labor and do all your work, but the seventh day is the Sabbath of the* LORD *your God. In it you shall do no work: you, nor your son, nor your daughter, nor your male servant, nor your female servant, nor your cattle, nor your stranger who is within your gates. For in six days the* LORD *made the heavens and the earth, the sea, and all that is in them, and rested the seventh day. Therefore the* LORD *blessed the Sabbath day and hallowed it*" (Exodus 20:8-11). The account in Deuteronomy 5 adds one more line to the Fourth Commandment: "*And remember that you were a slave in the land of Egypt, and the* LORD *your God brought you out from there by a mighty hand*

and by an outstretched arm; therefore the LORD *your God commanded you to keep the Sabbath day"* (Deuteronomy 5:15).

The language is plain and clear. Israel was to rest on the Sabbath day which began for them at sundown on Friday and lasted until sundown on Saturday. Taken literally, as addressed to an agricultural society, this commandment does not seem to apply to our technological, urbanized way of living. After all, Christians since the first century A.D. have used a different day of the week than this commandment mentions. We set apart Sunday, the first day of the week—not the seventh—for worship. Even though we often use the word *Sabbath* in our hymns and poetry as a synonym for Sunday, there really is a difference in the New Testament and the Old Testament worship or Sabbath-keeping practice.

Before going further, there is a significant fact that needs to be introduced here. The Fourth Commandment is the only commandment not repeated, enlarged upon, or made more stringent in the New Testament. There is no record that Jesus urged anyone to keep the Sabbath. In fact He often criticized the legalistic and unloving way in which it was being kept in His own day. He Himself was frequently accused of being a Sabbath-breaker (John 5:18). One incident recorded in Mark 2:23-28 related how the Pharisees, who were watching Jesus' every move, saw him letting His hungry disciples pluck ears of grain from stalks in a field to eat on the Sabbath. When they confronted Him with the fact that such activity broke the Sabbath prohibition against doing any work, Jesus responded: *"The Sabbath was made for man, not man for the Sabbath."*

Not only in the recorded sayings of Jesus, but later, in the writings of the apostles, no word was given about traditional Sabbath-keeping either. Surprisingly, the reverse is true. Paul wrote to condemn the legalistic Sabbath-keeping of his peers: *"You observe days and months and seasons and years. I am afraid for you, lest*

I *have labored for you in vain"*(Galatians 4:10,11), and, in another epistle, *"... So let no one judge you in food or in drink, or regarding a festival or a new moon or Sabbaths, which are a shadow of things to come, but the substance is of Christ"* (Colossians 2:17). At the first great church conference in Jerusalem, recorded in Acts 15:19-24, several instructions were sent back to the newly converted Gentile Christians; however, there was no mention of keeping the Sabbath. In fact, the two most-Jewish books in the New Testament, James and Hebrews, make no mention of the Sabbath at all. Moreover, in all of the lists of New Testament sins that appear from time to time in the gospels and epistles, Sabbath-breaking is never mentioned.

In light of all this, are we to ignore the Fourth Commandment now? The answer is no because, while the New Testament does not reiterate the exact details of the Sabbath commandment, it does in many places uphold the divine principle behind its words. Let us examine that principle. **A specific and proportional amount of time is to be hallowed or set apart for rest and worship**. In fact, the Hebrew word *shabath* from which we get Sabbath means to cease, desist, or interrupt activity.

> **This principle of one day in seven for rest was in force long before it was etched on a stone tablet at Sinai.**

The divine principle was not given first in Exodus or Deuteronomy. It was first given in the opening chapter of Genesis. God Himself rested after six days of creative labor. Later, in the wilderness journeys of Israel before they received the Ten Commandments at Sinai, the Sabbath principle was demonstrated in the giving and gathering of manna. On the sixth day the people were to gather a double-portion of the manna because none would appear on the seventh day. The Sabbath principle then, in its simplest definition, declares that man needs one day of rest and worship for every six days of labor, and this principle was laid out even before the Ten Commandments were given.

Very soon after the Ascension of Jesus, the first century Christians discarded the literal observance of a seventh day Sabbath while still keeping the Sabbath in principle. They stopped celebrating a Saturday Sabbath and instead began to set apart the first day of the week—or Sunday for this purpose. Many believe that this was because Christ rose from the dead and made His first post-resurrection appearances on Sunday. Paul seemed to accept this as the common practice when he was teaching in the last half of the first century A.D. In speaking about regular offerings to be received, he followed his great resurrection chapter of First Corinthians 15 with this: "*On the first day of every week, let each of you put something aside...*" (1 Corinthians 16:2). A couple of decades later John wrote in Revelation 1:10: "*I was in the Spirit on the Lord's day....*" What a wonderful name for the Christian Sabbath—the Lord's Day! So, it is believed that setting aside one day in seven was a continued practice of the first century church after the Ascension of Jesus. However, what is the place of the Sabbath principle in our lives today?

First, we must understand that when God rested after six days of creative labor as recorded in Genesis, He was illustrating a truth about the need for regular physical rest and spiritual renewal. This truth is stated along with the Fourth Commandment in Exodus 20:11 "*... For in six days the LORD made the heavens and the earth, the sea, and all that is in them, and rested the seventh day. Therefore the LORD blessed the Sabbath day and hallowed it.*"

This principle is written into the very fabric of the universe.

There is a rhythm that pervades all of life: work and rest, work and rest.

This flows from the very heart of God Himself, and we who are made in His image most need to observe it. Farmers know that even the land must be rested and crops rotated to get the most from the soil. There are other rhythms to be observed all around us. Tides rise and fall, day alternates with night, and seasons cycle with cold and hot, wet and dry. The natural world demonstrates vividly the need for a season of fruitfulness to be followed by a season of rest. Trees and plants have no choice about this. God has built into them this Sabbath principle, but He has given us the ability to choose when we will work and rest. However, in the Fourth Commandment He gave the principle of the Sabbath, which if kept, will help keep us healthy and balanced physically, emotionally, and spiritually.

It is amazing to discover how this divine principle has been proven true over and over again. The Sabbath principle is written into our bodies and personalities. Dr. David Seamands related how Dr. Hagler of Switzerland conducted a series of experiments some years ago. He discovered that more oxygen is expended from our bodies in a day through toil than can be recovered in a single night of rest. He discovered that the day of rest during a week is necessary to recover the cumulative loss of oxygen in six days of labor. In proof of the emotional value of the Sabbath principle, Sir James C. Brown, a British doctor said this: "We doctors, in the treatment of nervous diseases are now constantly compelled to prescribe periods of rest. Some periods, I think, are only Sundays in arrears!"[8]

Another illustration can be found in the records of the French Revolution. In an attempt to break away from all ties to religion and the church, the new leadership tried to abolish Sunday. Their method was to establish a day of rest only after ten days of labor; however, it did not work. In spite of all their anti-religious feelings, they had to return to the Sabbath principle's ratio of one out of seven days for rest in order to maintain a healthy labor force.

In the Hennapin United Methodist Church in Minneapolis, Minnesota, there is a beautiful Ascension window in the sanctuary. It is a memorial, given some years ago in memory of the Hugh Galbreath Harrison family. In a brochure describing it, the story is told about the Harrison family and their participation in the California gold rush of 1850. They headed out west by wagon train, but being deeply committed Methodist Christians, they decided not to travel on Sundays. They kept that day strictly for rest, Bible reading, and worship. Of course, while they were parked on Sunday, scores of wagons passed them, and they were ridiculed with comments like, "Pious fools!" or "Get your gold in heaven! We'll get ours in California!" But, do you know what happened? The Harrison wagon train not only caught up with all that passed them, but they also got there first! As they passed wagon after wagon, they saw animals lame and broken down, while their animals remained sound and healthy. And it was the same with the people. This "gift of rest" God gave in the Sabbath principle runs throughout all creation as a time of healing and renewal.

Someone reading this may himself have experienced a time when an emergency situation arose in which no day of rest was feasible for a few weeks on end. In such situations, that person probably found after the crisis, that he needed more days of rest to recover than if the normal one out of seven had been taken. The body, mind, and spirit get over-tired without regular rest and, in a weakened condition, often succumb to physical or emotional illnesses. We should not be surprised that God's work-rest ratio outlined in the Fourth Commandment is the best pattern to follow.

Besides a physical need for rest, the addition of a phrase in the second giving of the law in Deuteronomy 5:15 offers a spiritual reason for Sabbath-keeping: "And remember that you were a slave in the land of Egypt, and the LORD your God brought you out from there by a mighty hand and by an outstretched arm; therefore the LORD your God commanded you to keep the Sabbath day." From this, it is implied that resting one day out of seven is to be a reminder of the eternal rest to which we are headed.

> **Just as Israel was finally freed from the oppressive slavery of Egypt and was told to observe the Sabbath as a reminder of what God had done for them, Sabbath-keeping for us is a reminder of what the Lord will do for us in eternity.**

We will finally be freed from the constraints of this world—time, decay, sorrow, and death—and enter into a satisfying rest with God forever. So, even if there were not present benefits to be had from obeying the Sabbath principle, the spiritual example set by our obedience to God is a testimony to those who notice that we believe we are headed for an eternal Sabbath with our God.   Consider the words of Jesus again here: "The Sabbath was made for man, and not man for the Sabbath. Therefore the Son of Man is also LORD of the Sabbath" (Mark 2:27-28). Jesus taught that the Sabbath was a gracious gift from God to man, not a burden to be borne with great deprivation or excessive rule-keeping. Our attitude should be this: whatever can be completed before the Lord's Day should be completed so that we might rest in body, mind, and spirit.

Of course there have always been extremes in handling this gift of Sabbath rest. Some have interpreted the Fourth Commandment to mean, "You shall not enjoy Sundays!" God never meant that. However, in our time the other extreme is the worse danger to us—forgetting the whole purpose for the Sabbath. It is not to be just a physical change of pace, but it is to be a day when worship is central. In order to appreciate anything—especially the grace and goodness of our Heavenly Father—every person needs to stop and remember. We need to count our blessings regularly, express our love to God, renew our commitment to His will, offer our resources for His work, and unite with family and friends to study, pray, and hold each other accountable before God. Such things do not happen by accident. They must be purposefully planned and carried out.

In Ezekiel 20:18-20, the prophet was told by God of another value of the Sabbath-principle. When one day a week is set aside to worship God and to rest from unnecessary labor, it then serves as a sign between God and man of their relationship in loving covenant. God told Ezekiel of the disobedience of Israel in this matter: "*But I said to their children in the wilderness, 'Do not walk in the statutes of your fathers, nor observe their judgments, nor defile yourselves with their idols. I am the* LORD *your God: Walk in My statutes, keep My judgments, and do them; hallow My Sabbaths, and they will be a sign between Me and you, that you may know that I am the* LORD *your God.'*" When we stop our lives and remember God, we come to know Him better and better. When we do not, we cease to grow spiritually, and our stunted growth will become apparent sooner or later in our everyday lives.

Here follows a strong but true statement: if we forget the

Sabbath, we will soon forget God. The following story from the early settlement of New York illustrates this. Barbara Heck came with some Irish Methodists to start a new life in the new world. They had been converted under the preaching of John Wesley when he had come to Ireland. However, in New York they found themselves far away from the influences that God had used in their lives in Ireland. Without a regular structured worship schedule, Sundays became just like any other day. They all began to drift away from the things of God. One Sunday, Barbara Heck felt prodded by God's Spirit. There was a lay exhorter in the group named Philip Embury. We would call him a lay speaker today. A card game was in progress when Barbara suddenly grabbed the deck from the table and threw it into the fire. She pointed to Philip Embury and said, "Philip, if you don't start preaching to us, we're all going to hell!" She knocked down every excuse he gave, forcing Philip Embury to do what he was gifted to do. He later became an outstanding church leader, regularly preaching on Sundays, and beginning the first Methodist church in New York. When the Sabbath was remembered and kept, the Christians were spiritually fed and the lost were brought into saving faith.

Some of us are called to be Barbara Hecks—to persistently show the need for an observance of the Fourth Commandment; others are to be like Philip Embury, stirred to lead the way in making it a day of real worship as well as a day of physical rest. In His goodness, God gave us the proper rhythm for a healthy life. One day in seven is to be used for His glory and our complete renewal. The wise will hear and obey.

The Fifth Commandment:

Honor Your Parents

T he Fifth Commandment is very special because it is the only commandment with a grand bonus promised to those who obey it. Read its words: *"Honor your father and your mother, that your days may be long upon the land which the* LORD *your God is giving you"* (Exodus 20:12 NKJV). The first four commandments clearly showed how our thoughts and actions were to be directed toward God, but this fifth one takes a different focus toward a vitally important human relationship—that of children to their parents. In our examination of this commandment we will see that it provides a solid foundation on which to build not only our family lives but also our relationships in the world at large. The Jewish *Talmud* stated, "When a person conducts himself by honoring his mother and father, God is heard to say, 'It is as though I were living with them and they honored me.'" Moses de Leon, a thirteenth century rabbi explained that one of the first reasons father and mother should be honored as God is honored is because "all three have been partners in thy creation."[9]

Many Scriptures emphasize this commandment. Exodus 21:17 is one of several that sounds quite severe: *"Whoever curses father or mother shall be put to death."*

It has been said that the value of something can be determined by the penalty demanded for its loss or destruction. If this is so, God has put an extremely high value on honoring parents.

There are many Bible proverbs that emphasize the high value God places on obedience to this commandment: *"If you curse father or mother, your lamp will go out in utter darkness."* (Proverbs 20:20). *"Listen to your father who begot you, and do not despise your mother when she is old."* (Proverbs 23:22). *"The eye that mocks his father, and scorns obedience to his mother, the ravens of the valley will pick it out, and the young eagles will eat it"* (Proverbs 30:17).

According to New Testament Scripture, Jesus also upheld this commandment in His life and teaching. In the account of His having been left behind in Jerusalem by His parents after the Passover visit when He was talking with the teachers of the law, the Scriptures record that He returned home with His parents and was obedient to them (Luke 2:51). At the wedding at Cana, Jesus performed His first recorded miracle in response to the request of His mother Mary that He help the hosts with their wine shortage. Three years later, while enduring the agony on the Cross that would result in His death, Jesus still had the presence of mind to secure the future care of His mother whom He had apparently been supporting. He entrusted her to the care of His beloved disciple John with these words: *"'Behold your mother!' And from that hour that disciple took her to his own home"* (John 19:27).

Mention of the Fifth Commandment also occurs in the teaching of Jesus recorded by Matthew in 15:4-6: *"For God commanded, saying, 'Honor your father and your mother'; and, 'He who curses father or mother, let him be put to death.' But you say, 'Whoever says to his father or mother, "Whatever profit you might have received from me is a gift to God" then he need not honor his father or mother.' Thus you have made the commandment of God of no effect by your tradition."* Jesus clearly upheld the Fifth Commandment and sharply criticized the way the religious Jews tried to get away from obeying it by saying they would give all their offerings to God, thus excusing themselves from the clear command to care for their parents.

Since this command to honor our parents is clearly still in force today, how do we go about obeying it? **First, we must express gratitude to our parents as long as they live.** After all, they gave us birth and cared for us during the period of our greatest dependence. However, in the popular and modern pastime of assigning blame, many are often encouraged to delve deeply into their childhoods to discover all the things that their parents did wrong in their upbringing.

> **Certainly mistakes were made and sins committed by every parent who ever raised children, and we may have some legitimate emotional or even physical problems to prove our own sad cases. Yet the commandment still stands. We are to honor our parents whether they deserve it or not.**

There have been no perfect parents and no perfect childhoods. Remember the first two people in Eden! Even Christians who consciously seek to serve God and follow His principles find that time and time again they succumb to the selfish principles of the old sin nature. We are all in need of forgiveness and so must give forgiveness even to our parents that we might then be free to move on to a place where we can honor them as God commands.

One regret I have in my own life is that I did not tell my parents as often as I should have of my great love for them and deep gratitude for the life they gave me. I have a memory of being with my father at lunch in Jackson, Mississippi, while I was serving the Leavell Woods Church there. We talked of many things and I had the perfect opportunity to tell him how much I loved and appreciated him, but I let the moment slip by. Not long afterward, he died suddenly. The opportunity was missed. Later on, when my mother spent her last months in a nursing home, I did try to tell her, but I do not think she could comprehend what I was saying. Oh, I urge people to go ahead and say those words to the ones who will be most blessed in the hearing of them. Show honor to your parents through expressions of gratitude while you have the opportunity.

Another way we can honor our parents is by obeying them. Read these words written by the apostle Paul: "*Children, obey your parents in the Lord, for this is right. Honor your father and mother, which is the first commandment with promise: that it may be well with you and you may live long on the earth*" (Ephesians 6:1-3). "*Children, obey your parents in all things, for this is well pleasing to the Lord*" (Colossians 3:20).

The Fifth Commandment requires children to honor their parents and in so doing lays the groundwork for a very important development in the character of those children: obedience. Children will learn obedience as they honor their parents. This will be the foundation for all respectful relationships in their lives. Obedience learned in the home will be followed by obedience to teachers, and later on to all other authority holders.

> **When obedience is not learned at home, all other institutions and societal groupings suffer from the inevitable disruption caused by that failure.**

A big truth observed from seeing the Fifth Commandment in operation is this: honoring parents preserves society. Obedience to parents is not only good for society, it is really the key to independence for the child. When a child can learn to accept authority and receive direction, he will thrive in all future situations. A respectful, humble, and teachable person of any age is a joy to direct and follow. His obedient attitude will free him from condemnation, punishment, and disciplinary actions that would limit his freedoms and slow down his own plans.

With the increasing life-expectancy in modern societies, many adults are finding themselves in the position of caring for aging parents for long periods of time. Some call themselves the "sandwich" generation—still needed by their children but pulled to care for their parents. For centuries large families in most cultures have been a cause for joy and praise because together family members worked to meet the needs of the young and the old. Children were seen as a help and a hope for the future. The Psalmist wrote: *"Like arrows in the hand of a warrior are the sons of one's youth. Happy is the man who has his quiver full of them!"* (Psalm 127:4-5). However, not all adult children are willing to make the sacrifice needed to show such honor. Ellsworth Kalas told of hearing his mother speak about an elderly person caught in dire financial need: "It is amazing that one woman can care for four children, but that four grown children cannot care for one woman."[10]

Support of parents in their time of need is a very practical application of the Fifth Commandment.

What about that promise to those who obey the command to honor parents?

Paul's comment on this teaches that when people honor their parents, they are actually caring for themselves: "*Honor your father and mother, which is the first commandment with promise: that it may be well with you and you may live long on the earth*" (Ephesians 6:2,3).

A story taken from Grimm's Fairy Tales teaches this truth in a stinging way.

> Once there was a little old man, with trembling hands and feeble eyes, whose uncertain table habits became increasingly offensive to the daughter-in-law with whom he lived, until one day, she complained vigorously to her husband, the man's son. She and her husband took the fumbling old man to a corner of the kitchen, set him on a stool, and gave him his food in an earthenware bowl. Now he was no longer troubling them by dropping his food. Now the tablecloth was no longer soiled by his trembling, fumbling hands.
>
> One day, as he trembled, he dropped the bowl and broke it. Now the daughter-in-law, angered, ceased being even moderately civil. "If you are a pig," she said, "you must eat like a pig! You must eat from a trough." And they made a little wooden trough, and he ate from it.
>
> The pride of their lives was their four-year-old son. One evening they noticed the boy playing with his wooden blocks. His father asked what he was building. He answered with a smile, "I'm making a trough to feed you and Mama out of when I get big."
>
> For a few moments the father and mother just looked at each other without saying a thing. Then they began to

cry. They went to the corner and led the little old man back to his place at the table. They gave him a comfortable chair, and they put his food on a plate. And never again were they really deeply troubled by the food he spilled or the dishes he occasionally broke. They had learned that in honoring a parent, they were actually taking care of their own future.[11]

Truly the foundation of our nation depends upon the home.

It is the most important institution—more vital than Wall Street, Capitol Hill, or the Pentagon. Traveling through housing areas, I am sometimes struck with the thought that in many of those homes our nation's future is being formed, for what happens there between parents and children will have an effect for good or bad on us all.

How can we help with the establishment of a solid foundation for children? First, we need to remember that children learn best by example. They are influenced more by what we do than what we say. This is very convicting to most of us. However, what they hear is still very influential. Many of the standards they adopt come directly from what they have heard from television, disc jockeys, rap groups, musicians, internet output, and their own peers. How can the negative words and actions bombarding them be counteracted? Schools, clubs, and social agencies may all help to some degree, but the real defense to evil is established when the Fifth Commandment is followed in each home.

Embrace this command and meditate on its promise. Honor parents because it is God's plan, because it has been proven through the ages to be absolutely essential to a healthy society, and because you yourself will most likely need the respect and honor it commands each generation to give. Parents are not perfect, but they are part of God's plan for our world. Forgive any past sins and begin with joy to honor the ones who claim you as their own.

The Sixth Commandment:

Do Not Murder!

The Sixth Commandment, as the five that preceded it, speaks in precise and pointed language: *"You shall not murder"* (Exodus 20:13). Using only four words, God establishes the sacredness of life. He commands that life be protected. Yet, why is such an important command placed sixth in the list? The explanation lies in this truth: until God has His rightful and preeminent place in our lives, we will be unable to deal rightly with human life—our own or our neighbor's. So the Decalogue begins with commands about putting Jehovah God before all other gods, shunning idols in every form, using His name with respect as well as effectiveness, and setting aside one day in seven for building a closer relationship with Him through worship and rest. When God is on the throne of our lives, when He is the primary focus of our attention, then we can begin to see human relationships—and everything else—in their proper perspective.

When a person has a defective or diminished understanding of God, he will also have a defective or diminished appreciation for life. History offers many examples of this. The evil ideas and actions of Adolf Hitler in Nazi Germany are a prime example. He persuaded his followers to accept the idea that individuals are only valuable as they can serve or improve the state. If a person were incapacitated mentally or physically by birth defect, illness, accident, or age, Hitler promoted the idea that that person should not be allowed to continue living and burden the state with his upkeep. This devaluing of life expanded to include persons of different races, religions, and nationalities which Hitler deemed inferior to his "master" race. Since Hitler and his followers had no clear view as to who God really was, they methodically murdered millions.

The King James Version translates the Sixth Commandment *"Thou shalt not kill,"* but a better translation of the original Hebrew word is *murder.* There is a difference in killing and in murdering. For example, an accidental death caused by a careless driver is different from a conscious and deliberate choice to end a human life. The difference lies in the heart motive for the action. But why does God hold life so sacred that He prohibits its being taken in a murderous act? Let us examine the principles underlying this commandment.

First, human life is sacred because God Himself created it. The psalmist put this truth into words in the following psalms: *"Know that the* LORD *is God. It is He that made us and not we ourselves, and we are His . . ."* (Psalm 100:3) and *"For it was You who formed my inward parts; You knit me together in my mother's womb. I praise You, for I am fearfully and wonderfully made"* (Psalm 139:13,14). A painting might be sold at a flea market for only a few dollars or a small bit of change, but if it should be discovered that the artist was one of great fame, it might resell for hundreds, thousands, or millions of dollars. The difference in value of something depends upon the maker of it. Therefore no person is a worthless piece of humanity because each person has been created by God Himself!

Human life is sacred because it is the very handiwork of our Creator God.

Another reason that human life is sacred and therefore protected by God is that people have been made in the image of God. After God had created the birds and fish and animals, He said, *"Let us make humankind in our image, according to our likeness . . ."* (Genesis 1:26,27). We have been made with the capacity to know God, fellowship with Him, and share His plan for His creation. The stamp of God on human beings is what makes them different from animals and fish and birds.

Besides His likeness, human beings have received His breath: *"Then the* LORD *God formed man from the dust of the ground and breathed into his nostrils the breath of life; and the man became a living being"* (Genesis 2:7). We share the very breath of God, so that when we embrace another person, we are embracing one made in God's image and containing a spirit breathed into him by the Creator of the universe. If we were to murder another person, we would violate the very handiwork and breath of God.

If murder is strictly prohibited by the Sixth Commandment, is killing of all kind in all situations included?

The understanding of this gets complex when we consider the actions of people during war. Some see all killing as wrong and even ask for exemption from active military duty due to "conscientious objection" to fighting that could result in the death of another. However, self-defense or defense of one's country in war is not seen as a violation of this commandment by most people. In fact, Israel was often told to fight her enemies in order to bring God's judgment on those who had refused to submit to the one true God. Joshua and David were both men of war who testified to being directed and empowered by God for the military actions they went forward to undertake.

> **Since life is sacred, it must be defended, and the act of killing in order to protect oneself or others from murderous efforts for no godly purpose seems to be allowed by Scripture.**

What about suicide? Does a person have the right to take his own life? Since suicide is premeditated, it falls under the prohibition of the Sixth Commandment. While God is the final judge of every human heart, it can be seen in a vast number of suicide cases that the person involved was desperately depressed, and at least momentarily beside himself emotionally, mentally, and sometimes physically. Nonetheless, suicide is wrong because it usurps a right only Creator God can hold—the right to determine when earthly life should end. Suicide is wrong, but yet suicide is not an unforgivable sin. Its tragedy lies in the fact that it is a permanent solution to what was often only a temporary problem. It leaves behind great grief and guilt in the loved ones continuing to live because they often wonder what they could have done to prevent such a desperate act. It solves nothing and fails to give God His rightful opportunity to heal, comfort, strengthen, and restore. Obedience to the Sixth Commandment in the matter of suicide would save untold grief to family and friends and give opportunity for the power of God to be shown in solving serious problems or giving sustaining power to endure terminal ones. Disobedience to the Sixth Commandment through suicide gives no glory to God or grace and help to the suffering ones.

The most blatant breaking of the Sixth Commandment right now occurs some four to five thousand times a day in the United States; it is abortion. No issue since slavery has caused such division among good people. It deserves a chapter to itself, but a summary of the major issues will be attempted here. The most important question that must be asked is this, "What is it that lives within the womb after conception?" Is it, as supporters of abortion say, only an extension of the mother, no more sacred than an appendix or a tonsil? If the fetus is not a living human being in the womb, but simply a grouping of cells connected to the mother, then it is not wrong to remove and stop its growth. However, if the living cells are actually a separate human being, then premature removal to stop their growth is murder and a direct violation of the Sixth Commandment.

Here I will give my personal story as to how I woke up to the problem of abortion. When I was in seminary, abortion was not an issue. That fact reveals my age! Very seldom was it even mentioned. But when I began my ministry, it had begun to be seen by society as an option to be considered. One day a widow came to see me in a serious dilemma over a son whose girlfriend was pregnant. He was just out of high school, and although they had planned to eventually marry, it was not an ideal time at present. They were trying to decide what to do about this unexpected baby now on the way. Neither family involved had much money. The birth of the baby would cause many problems financially as well as in the planned education of the widow's son. I answered her plea for advice by laying out three options: "First," I said, "they can marry, get a job, and do their best. Second, they can put the baby up for adoption after it is born, or, third, the pregnant girl could have an abortion." I was soon moving to another church, but I learned later that they decided to marry, keep the baby, and do what they could.

Three or four years later, I went back to that church for some special event. While I was there, this couple brought their beautiful daughter to me. It was a solemn moment in my spiritual life. I thanked God that they had not taken my suggestion about having an abortion. Seeing that precious child before me, the issue of abortion suddenly became something very important to me.

I saw how the "choice" I offered could have ended the life of the precious child standing before me.

Sometime later, a professor from the Reformed Seminary came to my office. He was visiting pastors and inviting them to attend some sessions dealing with abortion. I attended. The insights from those sessions opened up a whole new world for me. He presented medical findings about the fetus at various stages of development in the womb. Those sessions convinced me beyond a doubt that the fetus was more than a potential human being; he was a human being with potential! I saw that the only thing that changed in that developing fetus at his birth was his life support system. He would go from receiving oxygen and nutrients through his umbilical connection to his mother to receiving it with his own lungs and mouth from the world into which he was born. I came to believe with deep conviction that abortion is murder.

Like suicide, abortion is not an unforgivable sin, but it is again a permanent solution to only a temporary problem. How we need to study God's word and stand firmly in our keeping of the Sixth Commandment! There may be extreme situations in which a person could justify such an action, although I have not yet seen one, but woe to anyone and any nation that fails to value every stage of human life!

Tragically, the legalization of abortion in our nation has been followed, as many predicted, with an acceptance of assisted suicide or euthanasia for the elderly or severely ill. Devaluation of life at any level opens the door to devaluation of life at every level. There is documentation of cases now where the sick or elderly are euthanized against their will or made to feel guilty if they refuse such intervention. All this results from a desensitized conscience about the sacredness of human life as established by this Sixth Commandment. I really believe that the speed with which our nation is rushing down the path of self-destruction is directly related to how this command to do no murder is being disregarded.

We have examined many things about the Sixth Commandment, but we have not yet looked at what Jesus had to say about it. First, Jesus revealed the real source of murder. Talking to the Pharisees in John 8:44, Jesus said: *"You are of your father the devil, and the desires of your father you want to do. He was a murderer from the beginning, and does not stand in the truth, because there is no truth in him . . ."* As New Testament Christians, we must realize that Satan delights in using human beings to destroy human life. When you participate in murder, you are serving the ends of Satan, not of God.

Jesus further commented on the Sixth Commandment by revealing that it involved more than evil actions; it began with evil thoughts in the heart of the murderer in the form of ungodly anger. *"You have heard that it was said to those of old, 'You shall not murder, and whoever murders will be in danger of the judgment.' But I say to you that whoever is angry with his brother without a cause shall be in danger of the* judgment. And whoever says to his brother, 'Raca!' shall be in danger of the council. But whoever says, 'You fool!' shall be in danger of hell fire" (Matthew 5:20,21). Jesus made it clear that the Sixth Commandment can be broken by a murderous attitude as well as by an act of violence. He makes us ask ourselves, "Is there something of a murderer in me?" Jesus would have us guard even our thoughts and intentions toward others.

An example of this comes from my experience as a pastor in conducting the funerals of parents whom I knew to have grieved over a wayward son or daughter. The child in each case had been selfish, thoughtless, and careless. The people who knew the deceased parent best would remark, "His (or her) life was shortened by the heavy concern for that rebellious child!" We can be guilty of taking the life of those who love us by our rebellion against God.

Ellsworth Kalas described a girl from a very poor family. She dreamed of going to college and becoming a teacher. But her parents and neighbors were very poor, not only financially, but also in their perceptions and expectations. They laughed at her dreams: "You a teacher?" they said, "And maybe you'd like to be president of General Motors, too!"[12] So they killed this girl's hope for her future, and in so doing, they killed something of the girl herself. I think that is what Jesus was saying when He said it was murder to insult someone or to put someone down. When this is done, something dies within that person, because human life is not only sacred, it is delicate.

All of this points to what the apostle Paul says about the law of God. It is a school-master to bring us to Christ.

We have all broken the Sixth Commandment according to New Testament interpretation. We have had murderous attitudes and have spoken poisonous words. We must seek the forgiving and cleansing power that Christ offers.

When *"thou shall not murder"* is considered carefully, its greatest application to our lives is not just a negative—to refrain from murder in attitude and action—but a positive: we must promote, encourage and embrace life with all of our heart, soul, mind, and strength. When I think of the people who have built up my life, I am grateful beyond words. Does that mean that I have never been put down by the comments of others? Of course I have, and those things hurt me and diminished part of my life. However, far more often I have had my life enriched by others through many kindnesses. I believe that these have lengthened and strengthened my life.

I think of Hattie Ferris, my elementary Sunday School teacher who wrote me letters of encouragement until her death, long after I became a pastor. I think of Fred Todd, who in my earliest days of ministry, told me the first Sunday I preached at the church he attended, "Every time you preach, I'll be back there in my place praying for you!" His encouragement and prayer support made me feel that I could serve God as a pastor.

So, just as cruel words and actions can deal death to something in us, kind words and actions can enrich and empower our lives. A friendly wave, a warm handshake, an encouraging telephone call, a comforting hug, or a thoughtful note brings to the recipient a healing touch, a hand up in a world where too often people are pushed down. Christians ought to bless constantly the lives around them, affirming the eternal qualities that lie dormant and helping others find the deep, full, and exciting possibilities of life on this planet. The effects are reciprocal. We enrich our own lives when we seek to bless the lives of others. We hurt ourselves when we fail to help others.

God gave this Sixth Commandment to promote, protect, and bless life—our own as well as the lives of others. As we obey it, we will surely experience its benefits as well as appreciate the wisdom of God in setting it forth to make our lives better.

The Seventh Commandment:

Do Not Commit Adultery

If it were put to a poll, this Seventh Commandment, *"You shall not commit adultery"* would be shown to be the most unpopular commandment of all. At this time in our culture, it is under the heaviest criticism. There is a tremendous assault philosophically and theologically from almost every area of modern society upon its simple prohibition, *"You shall not commit adultery."*

What is adultery? In the Old Testament, the Hebrew word for *adultery* originally meant "adulteration," which is defined as making something impure or of lesser quality by adding improper ingredients. This word *adultery* was first used in association with idol worship. The nation of Israel was constantly adulterating or adding unholy activities to the pure worship of Jehovah, her covenant God. However, the Seventh Commandment uses the word *adultery* to relate to the adulterating of the sexual relationship between man and woman who are united in the covenant of marriage. Adultery is the defacing or destruction of a relationship by having sexual relations with someone other than your spouse. The original and intended purpose for sexual intimacy was as a pleasurable bonding between one man and one woman within the covenant of marriage. The New Testament speaks out strongly not only against adultery, but also against fornication which would be any sexual relationships entered into outside the bonds of marriage. The biblical stance is that we are called to practice sexual faithfulness within marriage and sexual abstinence outside of marriage.

Despite the Bible's clear teaching, there is a complacency and casualness about adultery that is rampant in our modern era. To be sure, it is still the cause of gossip when it happens to someone we know and grief when it happens to us, but it no longer shocks us as it did our ancestors. And isn't the measure of a culture's moral purity assessed by examining what causes it to be shocked?

An example of this can be seen in a study of the dreaded disease mentioned so often in the Bible, the disease of leprosy. The root problem of leprosy is not that the disease itself causes deformity and infection of the body's extremities, but that it causes a loss of feeling or nerve sensitivity in the victim's skin. As a result, the leper may burn, cut, or otherwise injure a hand, foot, or other body part and not know it because the sense of feeling is gone. Then, the leper goes on to do further damage to it instead of protecting and treating it, with the continued use resulting in infection, broken bones, and finally the loss of function—all because of an inability to feel the original injury. The sense of feeling is the physical body's defense mechanism. In the same way, a sense of shock or spiritual pain is our protection against knowingly and continually breaking God's commandments. When our sense of shock is deadened by repeated exposure to sin, we lose our defense against it and much damage results.

To understand the seriousness of the sin of adultery, one needs to review and remember the underlying principles of a godly marriage relationship. First, marriage was invented by God

Himself as a gift to man and woman. Genesis 2:24 states, *"Therefore a man shall leave his father and mother and be joined to his wife, and they shall become one flesh."* If we only see marriage as a civil contract involving a wife, a husband, and the state, as the marriage license suggests, then it is strictly an earthly matter, like a legal business transaction. But if we see marriage as a holy covenant involving a wife, a husband, and God, then there is a sacred aspect of marriage that causes a more careful protection of its bond.

In the Old Testament, the breaking of a marriage covenant by an act of adultery was seen to be so grievous to God and so damaging to society that it required the death penalty to punish it. Through the execution of those committing adultery, the nation was to be purged of its evil effects.

> **To God, adultery is not just a private matter concerning two consenting adults, but a public matter recognized as an assault on the whole community because the bond of marriage is the foundation for a healthy society at large.**

Jesus fulfilled the law's requirement that adulterers be executed, as well as bearing every other penalty we deserve, through His death on the cross, but the moral law's requirement is still in effect. There are still moral and spiritual consequences which result from breaking this commandment.

An ancient bit of literature that many struggled to understand in their high school or college English classes makes an interesting point about the Seventh Commandment. The Parson in one of Chaucer's *Canterbury Tales* points out that the commandment outlawing adultery comes between the commandments prohibiting murder and theft. This, he explained, is because adultery is both the greatest theft and the greatest murder. It is a theft of the spouse's body and a murder of the "one flesh" union of man and wife. The Parson went on to argue that when a woman entered an adulterous relationship, she was stealing her body from her husband while also stealing her soul from Christ. He even compared it to someone sneaking into a church to take the Communion chalice, because the human body is the temple of the Lord, and adultery is a defilement of God's vessel of grace.[12]

Chaucer's insights were certainly founded in Jesus' teaching that from the beginning God had intended one man to wed one woman for life. They were to become one flesh in sexual union and what *"God has joined together, let no one separate"* (Matthew 19:6).

Adultery is wrong not only because it dishonors God's gift of marriage, but also because it distorts the biblical view of the human body.

Greek philosophers viewed the body and soul as enemies. They taught that the body is evil while the soul is holy. But Scripture views body and soul as one. We have a body and soul, but we also are a body and a soul. The Scriptures give a high place to the human body. Paul said emphatically in 1 Corinthians 6:18-19: *"Shun fornication"* because our bodies are the *"temple of the Holy Spirit."* Further, we are not our own, because we have been *"bought with a price."* Contemporary culture protests, "This is my body and I can do with it what I want to do!" But Scripture insists,

"Your body is God's body because He created it to be a dwelling place for His Spirit."

Since Scripture teaches that the human body is good, sexual intimacy is God's good gift to marriage. In fact, Biblical writers, inspired by the Holy Spirit, saw the sexual union between husband and wife as such a good thing that they used it to compare the Christian's relationship with God. They saw sexual intimacy as the highest level of communication between a husband and wife. That explains the use of the word *knew* when describing the sexual relationship of two spouses. In Genesis 4:1 it was written, "*Adam knew his wife Eve.*" In Genesis 4:7 it said again, "*Cain knew his wife and she conceived . . .*" The Bible thus portrays sexual intimacy as more than physical; it is also emotional and spiritual.

Is it not a known fact that physical touch provides some of our deepest communication—the embrace of a friend in sorrow, the reassuring grip of our hand by a spouse, or the soft hands of a baby touching our face? The Scriptures do not separate the physical and spiritual because they are bound together in what we call the human soul.

If we were purely physical creatures like dogs or cats, adultery would not be an issue. But, according to Genesis 1, the breath of God is in our mortal frames. One of the tragedies of modern culture is that so many are ignorant of this. Human beings are made in the image of God and have had His spirit breathed into their beings. We are far above the animal world. What we do physically affects us spiritually and emotionally as well. That is why adultery is such a serious matter to God and so devastating to the betrayed partner.

None of God's commandments are arbitrary rules without real-life application. They are not picayunish restrictions from a petty divinity. They are not the harsh demands of a tyrant who enjoys seeing us miserable. Instead, each one has been given to assurRe us of finding the best life possible. Adultery is wrong and prohibited by God because it does not allow us to be the healthy, happy, and holy people He intended us to be. When we betray another, we are plagued with guilt, and even if we confess and are forgiven, we will have scarred ourselves and others by the sin.

At a former pastorate in the 1980s, a fellow asked me to meet him for lunch. He told me his problem. He was attracted to a young divorcee at the office, and she was attracted to him. Nothing physical had happened, because he had been struggling with his Christian convictions that kept popping up alongside his emotions. But the pressure was mounting and the temptation was increasing. We talked and we met again. I told him everything I knew about the right and wrong of this situation. Finally, I said, "Think about your life twenty-five or thirty years in the future. Think of how proud you will be of yourself. Think of looking in the face of your wife or three children and saying, "I'm glad I said no to that temptation and yes to my commitment to you and to Christ." He took the challenge and helped instigate a transfer of this pretty young thing to another office in another town. I saw him a few weeks ago. He told me about his family, what his wife was doing, about his three children and their spouses and even his six grand-children. He went on and on about how he and his wife were enjoying the grandchildren. Nothing was said about our long-ago lunch sessions nineteen years ago, but I am sure he remembered them. I know I did, and I rejoiced that he had learned that adultery just does not work.

> **Giving in to momentary pleasure results in a lifetime of grief. Exercising self-control in obedience to God's command against adultery can yield a life-time of joy and peace and a freedom from grief and guilt.**

There will be people reading this who have already failed to keep this commandment. Is there a way back from adultery? In Jesus Christ there is. It is the way of grace. Adultery is a sin that affects many people, but yet it is still within the power of God to forgive it, just as He forgives every sin we confess. A statement by Paul in 1 Corinthians 6:9-12 sheds light on this: *"Do you not know that the unrighteous will not inherit the kingdom of God? Do not be deceived. Neither fornicators, nor idolaters, nor adulterers, nor homosexuals, nor sodomites, nor thieves, nor covetous, nor drunkards, nor revilers, nor extortioners will inherit the kingdom of God. And such were some of you. But you were washed, but you were sanctified, but you were justified in the name of the* LORD *Jesus and by the Spirit of our God"* [emphasis added]. Paul was speaking to believers here. This letter began with an address to *"those who are . . . called to be saints."* He recognized that they had sinned in many ways but had received the forgiveness of Christ and so should now stay clear of all sin.

The first four commandments described our proper relationship with God, the fifth, with its command to honor parents, established the home, the sixth prohibited all murder, and this seventh is placed perfectly to follow. When a home is established because parents are honored, the worst thing that could be done would be to murder one of its members, because that would rob them of the physical presence of the beloved. However, committing adultery is another way of murdering a family. It undermines the bond of marriage by dissolving the mutual trust and respect of spouses and destroys the emotional support and godly example needed by the children.

The God-given sexual desires experienced by people will not be satisfied long-term in any relationship other than marriage. The Seventh Commandment was given to save people from grief, frustration, and judgment. Obedience to it will bring joy to spouses, security to children, and a solid foundation for society as a whole. As with all the commandments, our Father knows best! Obedience to this one requires vigilance and commitment. We are not to linger near sexual temptation of any kind. Paul wisely commanded, *"Flee sexual immorality. Every sin that a man does is outside the body, but he who commits sexual immorality sins against his own body"* (1 Corinthians 6:18). The desires of the body wield a strong influence over us. However, God has given His Holy Spirit to all who ask, and that Holy Spirit will provide the strength to deny the inappropriate pleas of the flesh so that we can remain faithful to God and keep His life-saving and life-improving commandments.

The Eighth Commandment:

Do Not Steal!

Т

he Eighth Commandment, *"You shall not steal,"* legislates a
great and godly virtue—honesty. Though phrased in the
negative, this commandment points those who obey it toward a
very positive goal: keeping truth central in all words and actions.

Like the Sixth Commandment, this eighth one is quite
short—only four words—but in clarity it stands alone. On the
surface no explanation of it even seems to be necessary since
stealing means the same today as when this command was first
given: to take something that belongs to someone else without
their approval.

The Old Testament prophets were severe in their condemnation of stealing. Ezekiel condemned the nation of Israel for her
disobedience and included this specific charge in his complaint:
"The people of the land have practiced extortion and committed robbery"
(Ezekiel 22:29). Amos cried out, *"'They do not know how to do right,' says
the Lord, 'those who store up violence and robbery in their strongholds'"*
(Amos 3:10). Isaiah pointed out stealing as a real sign of
Jerusalem's degenerating leadership: *"Your princes are . . . compan-
ions of thieves"* (Isaiah 1:23). Wherever robbery was rampant, the old
prophets recognized that the people had neglected to maintain

their right relationship with God.

The New Testament writers had much to say about the evil of stealing, too. Paul clearly told the Ephesians that stealing was not to be part of the Christian life: *"Thieves must give up stealing; rather let them labor and work honestly with their own hands"* (Ephesians 6:10). In his warning to the Corinthians about who would miss the kingdom of God, Paul included "thieves" and then repeated in the same verse "robbers"(1 Corinthians 6:10).

One day when I was a small boy I went with a friend to the grocery store. As we left, Charles grabbed an apple from off the pile near the door and shielded it with his body. But Mrs. Boykin, the store clerk, had quick vision. She caught a glimpse of what he had done and called his name. Apples were cheap back then, not over a nickel. She was a kind lady, and had he asked first, she would have probably given him the apple. But she saw a destructive trait showing up in my friend, and she knew that it needed to be exposed. Stealing an apple could lead to a more serious crime later. The look of shame on my friend's face at getting caught will be one that always stays with me.

Stealing, whether something as insignificant as an apple or as expensive as a diamond necklace, is a terrible wrong in God's sight. Such an act violates the God-given right of private ownership.

> **You see, there is a positive side to the Eighth Commandment: people are allowed to have personal possessions. This is part of God's plan for an ordered society.**

The allowance of private ownership is necessary if we are to be good stewards of God's creation. We cannot control what we have no authority over. Therefore, God has allowed private ownership of many things so that the responsibility to care and share them can be carried out faithfully by the person having ownership. For example, if your right to own a home and a car is allowed under God's law, then you are responsible for using them to His glory. If they were not yours, you could not offer them for His purposes. The right to private property is granted by the Eighth Commandment, but the responsibility that goes along with ownership is taught throughout all Scripture. God requires faithful stewardship of those possessions according to His direction. Stealing ruins God's plan for individual responsibility in the area of stewardship and thus hinders the work of God's kingdom.

Stealing is wrong on other levels, too. It ignores the energy and time put into the acquisition of possessions and causes emotional pain as a result of the loss. Stealing is an act of selfishness. It disregards the needs, rights, and feelings of another while only seeking to satisfy the personal desire or lust of the thief. It also threatens the security of society. If every citizen constantly has to safeguard his possessions, there will be little opportunity or freedom left to serve one another as Christ instructed.

While stealing hurts its victims, as well as causing chaos in whole societies, it also damages the one doing the stealing. The thief loses the sensitivity of conscience. At first, the gentle inner voice might be disturbing, but with each repeated act of stealing that voice will become more and more muffled. The awareness of right and wrong will melt away whenever the moral monitor of conscience is disregarded. However, worse than what happens in the mind of the thief is what can happen in his spiritual relationship to God. The Psalmist recorded what every person who disregards God's law soon discovers: *"If I regard iniquity in my heart, the* LORD *will not hear me"* (Psalm 66:18). Stealing causes the guilty one to lose his most valuable possessions—self respect, a clear conscience, and a right relationship with God.

For generations men and women have trampled over the Eighth Commandment, but the sinful action is just as common today. Everything that has any value must be locked away. Homes and vehicles must be secured night or day, and even churches, once left open, are carefully locked up. In one section of a large city I saw porch chairs being chained to a post and fastened with a lock to prevent theft. In that same area I was told that shrubbery planted in the yard was at risk of being dug up and taken away by thieves. As a pastor I frequently hear of flowers being stolen from cemetery graves. Such blatant disregard for personal property increasingly disables our society, engendering fear, distrust, and cynicism.

The complexity of the problem is even reflected in the vocabulary developed to deal with it. Our courts have had to differentiate among the many acts of theft with such terms as petty larceny, grand larceny, fraud, embezzlement, or armed robbery. But new ways of stealing are constantly coming to light. Recently I read a news report about someone being arrested for stealing thousands of dollars from investors by manipulating the stock market via computer. However, this newer kind of robbery is just as damaging as that of the ancient farmer stealing his neighbor's sheep, even if the methods used now are more complex.

Perhaps we should bring application of this commandment closer to home by citing some more modern examples. First, let us consider the danger of using dishonesty to convince someone to make a purchase. Some examples follow. The turning back of the odometer of an automobile in order to enhance its appeal to a prospective buyer is a form of deliberate theft. Raising the price of necessary items during an emergency is an act of detestable theft against persons already victimized by tragic circumstances. Even pretending that a house is free from needed repairs because the structural damage is not in plain view is a form of stealing from a prospective buyer.

Other examples could be cited such as stealing time by being late, stealing resources for personal use that were intended for something else, or stealing wages from someone you have neglected to pay. However, the practice of stealing is as old as Genesis. The well-known story of Jacob and Esau reveals an attempt to take unfair advantage of another's predicament for personal gain. When Esau returned from the fields "famishing" from hunger, he asked his brother Jacob for some stew that he had made. Jacob had been plotting with his mother to take away Esau's birthright (the privileges that belong to the firstborn), and discerned he had Esau in the right place to drive a hard bargain. He said, "O.K., I'll exchange food for your birthright!" Foolishly, in his passion and haste for food, Esau sold his birthright for a bowl of stew. Later, Jacob managed to steal the blessing due to Esau, too. When Esau went to his father Isaac to receive the ancestral blessing, Isaac told him that Jacob had come "deceitfully" and had "taken away" his blessing (Genesis 27:35 KJV). Another rendering is that Jacob had "stolen" Esau's blessing! In today's highly competitive business world the temptation is always there to employ just this kind of "deceit" in making a deal. Some may laud it as a "smart business move," but it actually may be nothing more than common theft.

When Jesus drove "money-changers" out of the temple, it was not because they were selling poor pilgrims the birds they would need for their sacrifices. That in itself was a practical service offered to help people coming to worship and had been an allowable business for a long time in the temple courtyards. Jesus' anger was kindled at the way they were taking unfair advantage of poor people by overcharging them for the sacrificial animals. He cried out, "It is written, 'My house shall be called a house of prayer' but you are making it a den of robbers" (Matthew 21:13). Jesus put this practice of taking unfair advantage of people in the category of stealing.

Again, consider a common form of stealing called income tax evasion. That is a fancy title for income tax stealing. Stealing is stealing, whether it is from an individual, a corporation, or the government. We cannot excuse it as many do with the following explanations: "Oh, everyone does it." "Taxes are too high anyway." "They owe me some of this that I am keeping!" "I get paid in cash, so they can't prove I am cheating!" But Jesus said, "*Render to Caesar the things that are Caesar's, and to God the things that are God's*" (Mark 12:17). Paying taxes might be a bitter pill to take but it is our responsibility to do it honestly. That is what the Eighth Commandment requires.

We must also consider the danger we face in stealing through unearned or undeserved advancement. For instance, academic advancement is an area where thousands are guilty of stealing. Dr. David Seamands told about the president of a large southern university who received a letter from an outstanding alumnus. He had served as student body president while a student there and had later become successful in the business world. In the letter to the president, the alumnus had enclosed his diploma and this note: "I am no longer keeping something which does not really belong to me. I cheated in my senior examinations and did not pass them honestly. I stole my college education."

Not only can "honors" be stolen but also ideas or creative inventions can be taken from rightful owners. Writers, musicians, artists, and inventors are often targets of such theft. God wanted to protect individual investment of energy, ideas, and skills, and so predated copyright and patent laws with the Eighth Commandment.

> **To steal something whether tangible or intangible is a "shortcut" to success that God hates and never blesses.**

Finally, consider the danger we face in stealing from God. This is the most serious theft of all. Did you realize that the strongest language of condemnation by Jesus was directed at the failure to accept our duties as stewards for God? This can be seen in several of the parables of Jesus that address this subject. For example, in the parable of the talents, three servants were entrusted by their master with various numbers of talents. One had five, another two, and the last one was given one. Just one talent was worth more than fifteen years' wages, so each had been entrusted with more than any common laborer would dream about. Some time later the master returned and asked for an account of how the money had been used. The first two servants had doubled their talents, and they received high praise. The third servant had only hidden his talent, thinking at least to preserve it, but actually wasting its potential. Jesus said that the master condemned him with harsh words, *"You wicked and lazy servant!"* and then commanded that his one talent be taken away from him. He further ordered, *"As for this worthless servant, throw him into outer darkness, where there will be weeping and gnashing of teeth"* (Matthew 25:26-30). Other parables convey this same truth in the very strongest words. This sin of misusing what God has allowed us to possess as careful stewards makes us guilty of stealing from God.

We can also be guilty of stealing when we fail to offer a portion of our own material blessings for the work of God. The prophet Malachi lashed out against Israel about their failure to tithe. He asked, "*Will anyone rob God?*" The people asked how they had robbed God and were told, "*In your tithes and offerings*" (Malachi 3:8). In the New Testament our stewardship of material things includes everything that we have, so the tenth of our income should be the minimum that we return to God for His church and His kingdom advancement on earth. To refuse to give at least a tithe to God is nothing short of stealing. Someone quipped that just as Jesus was crucified between two thieves on a cross, so He continues to be crucified between thieves that steal what rightfully belongs to His kingdom. The greatest sin of America is to enjoy such immense prosperity while stealing from God. This will never continue without painful consequences.

We can steal in other ways besides withholding the resources that are rightly God's. We can fail to give God the commitment of our lives. Paul said to the Corinthians, "*Or do you not know that your body is a temple of the Holy Spirit within you, which you have from God, and that you are not your own? For you were bought with a price . . .*" (1 Corinthians 6:19-20).

The old story of the little boy whose father helped him make a toy boat illustrates this truth. The little boy took the boat to a steam to try it out. However, before he could grab the little boat, it was swept away by the current. With the father's help they searched down the stream among the overhanging limbs and weeds. Finally they found it, caught in thick intertwined branches. Excited with joy, the little boy held the boat close to his heart and said, "Little boat, you're mine. I made you and now I have found you. You are doubly mine alone!"

Our lives are rightfully God's first because He made us. Yet, He also endowed us with freedom to withhold our lives from Him. Our lives are also God's by the price paid for our redemption at the cross of Christ. Twice owned and yet still free to refuse to commit to His redeeming love. When we do refuse, we are stealing our lives from God's ownership. You see, when the New Testament asks us to surrender our lives to God totally and unconditionally, it claims that we are not being asked to give up anything that rightfully belongs to us. It claims to be merely asking us to return to the rightful owner what has always belonged to Him.

> **We are God's by both creation and redemption, and when we withhold our lives from God, we are stealing from the One who made us and purchased us from the bondage of sin at the cross.**

Paul wrote the Corinthians about the generous stewardship of the churches of Macedonia. He said, "... *they gave themselves first to the Lord* ..." (2 Corinthians. 8:5). That is where the cure for violating the Eighth Commandment begins. When we cease from stealing our lives from God's reign and ownership, then we find light and strength to overcome stealing in other subtle areas of life.

I challenge you to sit quietly and reflect on this commandment, *"You shall not steal."* Let the Holy Spirit reveal dishonesties in your life. Write them down so you will remember, and then get up and do something to right those wrongs. Begin by righting the wrong you have done to God. Return to Him with devotion, love, and commitment. Confess wrongs you have done to others and, if possible, make things right with them. Commit to living by His standard from this moment on. You will not be sorry, and the Holy Spirit will remind you and help you to obey.

The Ninth Commandment:

Do Not Lie!

A companion commandment to the call to honesty in the Eighth Commandment is the call to truthfulness in the Ninth Commandment: *"You shall not bear false witness against your neighbor."* The Contemporary English version modernizes it to read: *"You shall not lie about others."* This commandment was a clear prohibition against giving a false statement about someone in a court of law. But the Scriptures enlarge upon this simple commandment and make it apply to all human relationships. This is because God is a God of truth and, therefore, desires that truth be prominent in the character of His creatures.

This commandment, *"You shall not lie,"* probably puts the spotlight upon human nature more than any other commandment. When Adam and Eve committed the first sin, they were drawn to believe the serpent's lie, *"You shall not surely die . . ."* (Genesis 3:4,5), and from that moment to this, the most glaring result of the fall —the human separation from God—is the tendency to cover up with untruthfulness! So prevalent is this vicious trait that the psalmist David declared, *"I said in my consternation, 'Everyone is a liar'"* (Psalm 116.11). Paul wrote to Titus who was doing missionary work in Crete about this problem: *"It was one of them, their very own prophets, who said, 'Cretans are always liars . . .'"* (Titus 1:12). Even Jeremiah declared long ago, *"The heart is deceitful above all else; it is perverse—who can understand it?"* (Jeremiah 17:9). One of the biggest fruits of salvation, then, can be seen in the changing of the human heart from a disposition to lie in words and actions to a disposition to speak and live in truthfulness.

How blatantly people lie today! But should we expect anything else as long as "the evil one" reigns within human lives? Jesus said to some unbelieving Jews, *"You are from your father the devil . . . for he is a liar and the father of lies"* (John 8:44). Our own nation felt the pain of seeing the President exposed for bearing false witness in 1999. The top executive of our land lied, but worse than that, he was defended by many because what he had done was said to be merely what other leaders in government also do. The Ninth Commandment was pushed aside as just another rule that everyone has broken.

That is actually true—everyone has broken it, but the casual attitude toward lying is a great sin.

God's nature of perfect truth is set against all untruthfulness.

In Revelation 8 the penalty for lying is stated clearly: ". . . *all liars . . . will be in the lake that burns with fire and sulfur, which is the second death"* (Revelation 21:8). The writer of Proverbs had declared centuries earlier, *"Lying lips are an abomination to the Lord"* (Proverbs 12:22)

When rumors started that a popular head coach was being tempted with a better job offer, that coach assured players, alumni, and members of the media that he would not leave his current situation. He said, "There's nothing to these rumors. I 'm here to stay." However, shortly afterward, when he abruptly resigned to accept that rumored position, his earlier denials burned in the memories of thousands of supporters who perceived them as nothing less than premeditated lies. His lying was talked about, written about, and condemned by many because it had been so blatant. But that is the frightening thing about lying. It can be so deeply rooted in our sinful hearts that we can lie to others while deceiving ourselves that we are justified in doing so. This subtle deception is alarming.

Yet, some forms of lying are not subtle at all. We sometimes knowingly speak what we know to be false. How easily we get caught in unpleasant situations that seem to push us to lie in order to escape! Another reason we knowingly lie(we would rather call it "stretching" the truth) is to get attention, sympathy, or even just a laugh. However, the more we lie, the easier it becomes till eventually it develops into our normal way of speaking. We may get to the point that we can even lie without our conscience giving us a single pang!

Charlie Reese, a syndicated columnist, addressed the prevalent practice of lying. The main thrust of his column was the lying noted commonly in politics. He described two kinds of liars. First, there are "rational" liars who lie in order to accomplish a specific goal. For example, a campaign team trying to elect a certain candidate justifies spreading lies about their opponent's record, beliefs, or past conduct because they want their candidate to look better and be elected. A second group of liars, the "compulsive" liars, focus on the immediate moment, saying whatever is necessary to gain a perceived advantage for their purposes. Both types are a danger to themselves and others, and, sadly, even Christians can be guilty of these behaviors. Much like Reese's rational liars, we might "add" to the truth (i.e. lie) to promote our Sunday School class, church, pastor, or program over another to gain a member or just some recognition. Similarly, like the compulsive group, we lie simply to put forth a better image to others in ordinary conversations when no such lying is necessary or expected. Paul recognized this problem and wrote to the church at Ephesus: *"Therefore, putting away lying, let each one of you speak truth with his neighbor"* (Ephesians 4:25).

There is really only one way to rid ourselves of this dishonest behavior, and that is to confess the lie as soon as we realize it has been uttered. We must confess it to God and to the one to whom it was spoken. This is indeed a painfully humbling experience to have to tell someone, "I lied," but it keeps us sensitive to the voice of the Holy Spirit. That remembered pain will make us slower to lie again. The Holy Spirit longs to not only remind us of the truth, but also to clean out the lying and establish God's truth in its place.

How clearly I remember the letter I wrote from my college dormitory to a literature teacher whom I had had in the ninth grade. The Holy Spirit had been reminding me of a day in class when I lied to her. To finally clear my conscience, I wrote a letter of confession. She had assigned a book for all of us to read and on which we were to write a report by a certain date. I procrastinated and failed to finish the book on time, yet, when she called my name to ask about whether or not I had, I just lied and said I had. But, the Holy Spirit never let me forget that day, so five years later I wrote her to confess the lie. It was painful for me because she was a member of the church that my father pastored. However, my conscience was finally cleared, and I was left more sensitive to the importance of truthfulness.

Dr. David Seamands told about a young man who was extremely popular in his town and who, during revival services, was dramatically converted. He was a very successful salesman. A few weeks after his conversion, he was giving a sales pitch to a manager of a large company. The manager was on the verge of choosing between two products this company put out. Finally, he said to this salesman, "Dave, tell me, if you don't mind, which one of these products our rival, our biggest competition, purchased from you." The difference in commission on the two products was quite large, so Dave lied. He told the manager that his competitors had purchased the more expensive product, which they had not. So the manager signed a large contract for the better brand. Dave said the moment he picked up his briefcase and walked out the door, the Holy Spirit said in his head, "Dave, you lied!" He was crushed. He had been witnessing at his work and sharing the joy of his new life. But since his conversion, he was not alone. God's Spirit now lived within Him, and He was hurt by the lie Dave had told. A day passed and he could go no further in his guilt. The next day he made another appointment with the manager. He went back and said very humbly, "My life has been changed by Jesus Christ. Before that I was a colossal liar, and I lied to you yesterday. The company you asked about bought the cheaper product. I understand how you might feel about this, and in fact, you may not want to do business with a company who sends out a salesman like me. In case you do want to do business with my company, I'll send you another salesman. But I lied, and I'm sorry." As you might imagine, that company manager sat there dumb-founded, with his mouth hanging open. He was speechless. In the end, he was so moved by Dave's story that he kept the original contract.

Confession is not an easy thing. It can be extremely painful. But as James put it, *"Therefore confess your sins to one another, and pray for one another, so that you may be healed"* (James 5:13).

Only God can forgive sin, but when we have wronged another person, and in this case, lied to another, confession opens us up for God's power to heal the compulsion to lie.

Second, not only are we to guard against speaking what we know to be false, but we are to guard against another subtle form of lying: "coloring" the truth so that it takes the form of gossip. Gossiping or passing on the "truth" when such private information can hurt or embarrass someone should not be something done by Christians. Christian love demands that we ask ourselves first, "Even if this is true, is it necessary? Is it helpful? Would I want someone saying such about me?"

The Scriptures are specifically clear on this issue. From the letter to the Ephesians we hear this: "*Let no corrupt word proceed out of your mouth, but what is good for necessary edification, that it may impart grace to the hearers.*"(Ephesians 4:29 NKJV). Then in another epistle Paul gives Timothy instructions to be passed on to the younger widows lest they become "*idle, wandering about from house to house, and not only idle but also gossips and busybodies, saying things which they ought not*" (1 Timothy 5:13). Further discussion is found in Paul's letter to the Romans where he lists those who have "*a debased mind*" as including "*gossips*" and "*slanderers*" (Romans 1:29). Paul was not alone in noticing the problem. James wrote accurately when he noted: "*But no man can tame the tongue. It is an unruly evil, full of deadly poison. With it we bless our God and Father, and with it we curse men, who have been made in the similitude of God. Out of the same mouth proceed blessing and cursing. My brethren, these things ought not to be so*"(James 3:8-10).

A pastor who has been a close friend of mine made an innocent mistake in his church responsibilities, but what happened was spread among church members with the report being twisted and added to until his character was ruined. He was forced to leave the church which had crucified him with the gossip of half-truths and half-lies. How tragic to take part in such lying which can literally destroy the life of another!

However, it is not only with the lies of gossip that we can destroy others, but also with our silence. If we remain silent when someone's character is being tarnished, when we know that the report is wrong, or at least partly wrong, are we not helping to spread a lie? Clovis Chappell, in his book *Ten Rules for Living*, referred to a person who listens to gossip as a "fence." This term comes from the underworld thieving rings where the one who handles the stolen merchandise for the thief is called a "fence." Without a place to sell his goods, the thief would be out of business. So it is with gossip. There must be a person receiving the "goods" for gossip to be spread.

Silence is the same as approval when someone's reputation is at stake. The tongue can be deadly when it is moving, but it can also be deadly when it is still.

We have seen that through speaking lies or through silently receiving lies unchallenged we break the Ninth Commandment. However, there is yet another way we break it—by allowing our lives to be a lie. A living lie is the biggest lie. John, in his first epistle put this very simply, *"If we say that we have fellowship with Him, and walk in darkness, we lie and do not practice the truth"*(1 John 1:6).

The early church saw what it cost to live a lie in the sad attempt of Ananias and Sapphira to deceive the leadership regarding their offering. They had sold some property, and in keeping with the communal experiment of the young church, were expected to put all the proceeds into the common treasury. However, Ananias brought only a portion of the proceeds to the apostles, while claiming it to be the full amount. The Holy Spirit gave Peter the discernment to detect the lie and so he asked, *"Ananias, why has Satan filled your heart to lie to the Holy Spirit and to keep back part of the proceeds of the land. You did not lie to us but to God!"* With that, Ananias fell over dead. When Sapphira came in later, not knowing about what had happened to her husband, she was asked if the price given was the full price they had received for the land. She lied also and, like Ananias, fell suddenly dead. The rest of the account reported that a *"great fear seized all who heard of it"* (Acts 5:5). No doubt, the church became more deeply devoted to truth after witnessing the tragic end of the couple who were living a lie!

A person does not just suddenly start to live this kind of double-life, with one side lived before the public and another kept carefully hidden. Such deceit starts slowly and gradually takes hold. Soon, a person may become blind to the hypocrisy of his life. Consider this modern example. With the exponential expansion of the internet, many are addicted to on-line pornography, although they would never willingly let that be known. In public they continue to preach, teach, lead, love, or organize, while the secret life of the lie works its slow poison into the whole of their lives. When the prophet Jeremiah described the human heart and its capacity for evil as *"desperately wicked"* he also asked, "Who can understand it?"(Jeremiah 17:9). The implied answer is that no human can, but God sees to the core of each of us and knows about every single lie we try to hide.

Psychology has made many attempts to explain our deceitful ways. We are told that it is perfectly normal to put up "defense mechanisms" such as lying when we want to do something that would not be accepted or understood by others. Ignoring the God-given mechanism called conscience and failing to admit to ourselves that some action taken or thought followed is sinful, we gradually learn to turn off the warning system. But the apostle John declares that if we think we can have fellowship with God while walking in darkness, *"we lie and do not do what is true."* Continuation in a double-life will only result in self-deception with the result being that *"the truth is not in us"*(1 John 1:8).

In one of Charles Dicken's short stories, a young man is featured who left the simple ways of a small community for the city life. As time passed, he became a pick-pocket. This was a far cry from the life he had known in his younger days, but he had accepted it as necessary to his current existence. One day after picking a fat wallet, he looked across the street and saw a young lady with whom he had grown up as a child. He remembered how good and innocent she was and how good and innocent he had been in those long ago days back home. Dickens wrote that he leaned his warm forehead on the cold iron of a lamp post and sighed, "Oh, God, I hate myself!"

We were not created to live a lie—to walk in darkness. Within every person caught up in a life-style of deception there is the same realization, though often stifled or ignored, that on occasion cries, "Oh, God, I hate myself!"

We were created to live in truth, to walk in God's light. We were not created for the darkness. The Ninth Commandment offers hope for a life of truth. The way back to it begins with confession.

We must confess that God is true and that we have been living a lie. This will make room for Christ who is *"the Way, the Truth, and the Life"* to fill up our lives with Himself. By the Divine *"Spirit of Truth"* we are offered forgiveness and a new life (John 15:26). As we say "yes" to Him by faith, He drives out the *"self-deceit"* and sets up His reign of truthfulness. We can begin to live, as Bonhoeffer wrote, "in the atmosphere of truth." This is what God intended for us when He set the standard for truthful living in the Ninth Commandment. It is a standard He will empower you to meet if you will just let go of the lies and turn to Him.

The Tenth Commandment:

Do Not Covet!

In many ways, the Tenth Commandment is the greatest of them all! Certainly it is the greatest of the last six commandments which have to do with human relationships. No other set of ancient laws has anything like this last commandment. Read it in its entirety: *"You shall not covet your neighbor's house; you shall not covet your neighbor's wife, nor his male servant, nor his female servant, nor his ox, nor his donkey, nor anything that is your neighbor's"*(Exodus 20:17). This commandment goes deeper than any mere outward action to deal with an inner attitude. It goes below the deed to the disposition of the soul. It goes behind the hand to the heart itself. It is the most comprehensive of all the commandments. I believe that it comes last because the sin it warns against is the most treacherous of all.

What does it mean to covet? It is not easy to define. Does it mean to desire something? No, it has to mean more than that because our lives are made up of desires. Without them, we would not be fully human. We desire food because our bodies must have nourishment to survive. We desire companionship and love. We desire approval and respect. Such things give us a reason to get out of bed and wash our faces in the morning! We desire a job, a house, and a means of transportation. These are all legitimate human desires. So, human desires, if they are legitimate are not what constitutes covetousness.

Well, is coveting a desire for something we do not have? No, it is not exactly that either. If it were, we would need to close our schools, because millions desire an education they do not have. Almost everything we call progress, improvement, or civilization has come from some kind of desire for what is absent. Even in spiritual matters, desire is a legitimate response. In 1 Corinthians 12:31 Paul said, "But *desire* (or strive for—or, as the King James Version has it, *'covet earnestly'*) *the best gifts.*" Jesus even said, "*Blessed are they who hunger and thirst after righteousness*" (Matthew 5:6). So, a simple desire for something we do not have is not necessarily covetousness.

Christianity differs in this matter from some other religious systems. In Buddhism, for example, desire for material things is seen as the cause of all suffering, so the central thrust of that religious system is to destroy all desire. Buddhism calls for its followers to ignore the basic human desires, while the Bible teaches that God has provided us with a world of good things, and that He wants us to enjoy these things. So, legitimate desire, according to the Scripture, is not in itself wrong.

What is it then to covet? Defining covetousness is like trying to define "love." While it can be recognized when present it can still remain hard to describe in specific terms. A dictionary definition will probably get closest to its meaning. One source defines "to covet" this way: "to desire inordinately or without due regard for the rights of others." To covet means to desire what it is not right or lawful for us to have. It is not wrong to desire a spouse, a good employee, a house, an animal, or even a ticket to a big sporting event, but it is wrong to desire those things if they already belong to another.

The motive behind the desire is the problem in covetousness.

Normal desire gone wrong was at the very heart of the fall of humanity. The perversion of God-given desires, the "out-of-balance" pursuit of what is not rightfully ours is at the center of human depravity.

> **Covetousness involves greed and greed regards only self, ignoring the rights, dreams, and needs of others.**

Covetousness can be found in every culture. Proverbs about its dangers are found in every country's literature. A common adage in our culture claims "the grass is always greener on the other side of the fence." The ancient works of Aesop include a fable about a man who foolishly killed the goose which had laid golden eggs. The fable ended with this truth about the covetous spirit: "Much wants more and loses all." A proverb from Scotland observes, "The covetous man will never have enough until his mouth is filled with mold." Also, from India, comes this one: "When you mention money, even the corpse opens his mouth!" On and on could be quoted proverbs from around the world and from every age.

Covetousness not only affects every society, but every level of society. It even makes its way into the church. Some of the most promising ministers of the gospel have had the sharp edge of their ministries dulled by covetousness. You might have thought that mishandling of Scripture was your denomination's biggest problem—and that is certainly a wide-spread problem, but I dare say that covetousness in the hearts of ministers of the gospel is an even greater problem! In order to climb the ladder of ministerial success, servants of God frequently fall prey to compromising their message to gain human approval over the approval of Christ. I sincerely believe that one high-level church leader who did not care about personal popularity could cry out against the wrongs within his church and be effectively heard. But covetousness has crippled the witness and effectiveness of many leaders who *"loved the praise of men more than the praise of God"* (John 12:48).

Consider this, it is the spirit of covetousness that has broken every system of government devised by human beings. It is covetousness that has smashed every dream of humanity—from Plato's *Republic* to Thomas More's *Utopia*; from Marxist communism to, God forbid, our own American democracy. Our system has only survived thus far, in spite of Watergate and the recent Clinton scandals, because our system of government is not based on the idea that all people are basically good and virtuous, but instead based on a system that has placed safeguards within its structure to stop or at least slow down the damage caused by covetousness. The checks and balances placed in our system of government hinder the covetous actions of individuals and organized groups who would attempt to take full control. Thank God for the insight into fallen humanity held by our founding fathers!

Even in the smaller arena of family life, covetousness is devastating. Have you noticed how early it surfaces? Give a child a toy and he or she will be happy with that toy until another child comes along with a seemingly better, newer, faster model. Observe how the first child makes an attempt to get the second toy, too.

Covetousness begins with a sense of discontent which left alone will grow quickly into greed.

Jesus showed concern about the "heart condition" associated with acts of covetousness. His remarks emphasize the importance of the Tenth Commandment and its correlation of inner thoughts to outward actions. Luke records a time when someone brought a family dispute over an inheritance to Jesus to settle. He refused to settle it, but instead warned them of the root cause of their dispute with these words: *"Take heed and beware of covetousness!"* (Luke 12:15). Jesus was not against a fair settlement of the inheritance or any business matter, but He was underscoring the priority of a right attitude about material things. If something had to be sacrificed to settle the dispute, do not let it be the right inner attitude.

The apostle Paul, too, recognized the correlation of a covetous spirit with sinful activities. In a warning about sexual misconduct outside of marriage, he linked unholy actions with a covetous attitude. He wrote, *"For this you know, that no fornicator, unclean person, nor covetous man, who is an idolater, has any inheritance in the kingdom of Christ and God"* (Ephesians 5:5 NKJV). Paul recognized that any sin—like sexual misconduct—really has its beginning with a covetous thought, a desire to have what belongs to another. Sexual sin is coveting another's body for self-gratification, and that covetous attitude, when allowed to continue, ultimately leads to idolatry, making sexual pleasure one's god.

So, how can the struggle against covetousness be won? An important insight is offered in Psalm 37:4: *"Delight yourself in the Lord, and He will give you the desires of your heart."* I used to wonder what that meant, but now I think I know. If I make the LORD the central focus of my life so that I find my delight in Him, I will find my desires also met. But, the secret is this: if I walk with Him, trust in Him, seek His will above my own, I find that my desires are sifted, shifted, and cleansed by His Holy Spirit. I find that my "want tos" change; my desires begin to resemble His desires. When I desire what He desires, I receive the things I long for.

Jesus said it simply, *"Seek first the kingdom of God and His righteousness, and all these things will be given to you as well"* (Matthew 6:33). "Things" are helpful and good, but they should not be allowed to push God into second place. Paul wrote to Timothy that God . . . *richly provides us with everything for our enjoyment"* (2 Timothy 6:17), but before he said that, Paul warned that we should not *"set our hopes on the uncertainty of riches, but rather on God"* (2 Timothy 6:17a).

That is where we must begin in the struggle with covetousness. We must put our eyes on God, our faith in Him alone above all else, so that He might cleanse and rightly move our desires into an alignment with His. Ever-practical James wrote this: *"Draw near to God and He will draw near to you. Cleanse your hands, you sinners; and purify your hearts, you double-minded"* (James 4:8).

A key word we need to notice if we are to fully understand this Tenth Commandment is "neighbor." We are not to covet what belongs to our neighbor—the one next door, in the next county, or even on another continent. Loving our neighbor includes not being covetous of what he possesses. Love, according to 1 Corinthians 13:4, is not "envious." Isn't it strange how easily we are tempted to envy our neighbor because he has something we do not? But Paul also says, *"Rejoice with those who rejoice, weep with those who weep"* (Romans 12:15). Most of us have discovered that it is easier to weep with a neighbor than to rejoice with a neighbor. I suspect that the truest measure of friendship and of Christian love is our readiness to rejoice over our neighbor's gain, especially when that gain is the kind that we desire. Jesus said that we should love our neighbor as ourselves which would certainly include finding joy and fulfillment in his good fortune.

If I can rejoice in my neighbor's abundance, blessing, success, and rewards, I will enlarge and increase my own happiness.

> **Unselfish love is motivated by God and when allowed to surface, it will crowd out the small, mean spirit of covetousness which tries to develop within us.**

Covetousness shrinks my capacity for joy; while rejoicing in the blessings of another increases my ability to enjoy every good and perfect gift no matter who receives it.

Paul wrote, "*Godliness with contentment is great gain*"(1 Timothy 6:6). Contentment is the opposite of covetousness. Contentment is the gift of God to those who put Him first in their lives. To be content is to be right with God, with one's self, and with one's neighbor. Dr. Ellsworth Kalas, in his book *The Ten Commandments from the Backside*, describes the satisfying contentment observed by the fourteenth century saint Tauler of Strasbourg upon his meeting an unfamiliar beggar.

Tauler said, "God give you a good day, my friend."

The beggar answered, "I thank God I never had a bad day."

Tauler was silent for a moment and then added, "God give you a happy life, my friend."

And the beggar answered, "I thank God I am never unhappy."

Tauler was puzzled and asked, "What do you mean, 'never unhappy?'"

"Well," the beggar explained, "When it is fair, I thank God; when it rains, I thank God; when I have plenty, I thank God; when I'm hungry, I thank God; and since God's will is my will, and whatever pleases Him pleases me, why should I say I am unhappy when I am not?"

Tauler was now in awe of his new friend. "Who are you?" he asked.

"I'm a king," the beggar answered.

"A king!" exclaimed Tauler, now almost ready to believe it. "Where is your kingdom?"

The man in rags answered firmly but calmly, "In my heart, sir! In my heart!"

Obedience to "*You shall not covet . . .*" will introduce all of us into such a kingdom of contentment! May we all discover first hand what a vast and wonderful kingdom that can be!

The Law
and the Gospel

One more chapter is needed before we close this study of the Ten Commandments. This chapter will attempt to explain something not so easily understood: the relationship of the Old Testament law with the New Testament Gospel. Questions about this subject usually surface in one or more of the following forms:

1. **If no one can keep the law perfectly, why was the law given?**

2. **If we are saved by grace and not by keeping the law, why do we need to study the law?**

3. **When Jesus died on the cross, didn't the "day of the law" cease and the "day of grace" begin?**

To find a satisfactory answer for each of these questions, we will begin with some basic truths about the Old Testament law which the Ten Commandments so grandly set forth in summary form. First, we must recognize that the Old Testament law presents the wisdom of God in a medium that can be studied, memorized, discussed, and obeyed. This might not seem to be very important, but it is actually overwhelmingly generous of our God! Being the Creator of the universe, Maker and Keeper of all things, Source of all knowledge and power, God certainly did not need to "publish" His thoughts beyond the magnificent splendor visible in His creation. Yet He wanted to have a relationship with us. That could not happen unless there were a way for us to know Him personally. We could be afraid of His great power as seen in nature. We could be appreciative of His provision of air, water, food, and life in the cycles and seasons, but we could not have known Him, loved Him, or served Him in a satisfying way unless He revealed that way to us in a manner we could understand. The gift of the law to Israel and through Israel to the world has no equivalent in all history. God bent down to us and personally superintended the giving, recording, and preserving of His law so that we could know His plan for us and follow it. Obedience to Him brings blessing, and the Old Testament law revealed His wonderful wisdom for the living of our lives.

In light of their great revelation, it is shocking today to see the public display and discussion of the Ten Commandments so fiercely attacked. The American Civil Liberties Union claims to be for freedom of religion; yet, it has fought strongly to remove public displays of the Ten Commandments from courtrooms and public classrooms throughout our nation. But their removal from public view will never remove them from their place in the foundation of our lives. They are still the wisdom of God and powerfully applicable to our modern existence. Paul seemed to shout praise for them with this statement on their worth: "O, *the depths of the riches and wisdom and knowledge of God! How unsearchable are His judgments and how inscrutable His ways!*"(Romans 11:33).

In addition to proclaiming the wisdom of God, the law declares the goodness of God. Many who have read the Ten Commandments see only harsh directives, narrow boundaries, and crushing judgments in their prohibitions. Yet, when they were first given, Israel eagerly agreed to the covenant they set forth: "*Everything the* Lord *has spoken we will do*"(*Exodus* 19:8). Why? Because the people were convinced that the God who gave them was good! He had just delivered Israel from four hundred years of slavery in Egypt, and in so doing demonstrated His supernatural power in caring for them while defeating their enemies. They did not see the law as a grouping of restrictions to make them miserable, but instead as a set of instructions to make their lives good. The law reflected the good character of God.

But that's not all! The law not only displays the wisdom and goodness of God, but also illustrates the practicality of God. God put together a plan, a pattern for us to follow that would insure our having lives that are useful, meaningful, satisfying, and memorable. He—our Creator—knew how to make life work best. Leslie Flynn in his book *Now a Word from Our Creator* writes:

> The Ten Commandments may seem narrow, but so does every runway on airports around the world. Yet no passenger wants his pilot to miss the narrow runway and land a few yards off the mark in some field or waterway or row of houses. The narrow ribbon of pavement is really the broad way that leads to a safe, comfortable landing. So the seemingly rigid Decalogue guides us to happy, fulfilled living.

The Ten Commandments point to the practicality of God in showing us the way that life works best. We do not have to learn everything the hard way.

We do not have to try ninety-nine ways before stumbling on to the one that works.

God has done the work for us and presented us with a written book of directions for how to make the most of the life we have been given.

Besides revealing the wisdom, goodness, and practical direction of God, the law reveals our need for a Savior. The standard God sets forth in the law is a high one. All by ourselves, we could never meet the demands of the law. From the beginning God knew this and gave the law to Moses, but also provided a plan for sinners to approach Him for forgiveness when they failed to keep the law. A system of sacrifices was given so that man could come to God, not in his own goodness, but with the blood of a substitute, representing the heavy cost of sin and acceptable to God. The sacrifices were always meant to point man to Christ. Paul taught his Galatian congregation that the law, though it cannot save us, has always been good. Its high standard revealed how far off we really are. Its sacrificial demands prepared us for the one perfect and permanent offering of Christ Himself. The law was like a disciplinarian, or schoolmaster, to bring us to Christ (Galatians 3:24).

The Greek word for disciplinarian or schoolmaster is *paidagogos*. *Paido* (compare to the Latin *ped*) means *feet*. *Gogos* means *to lead*. A disciplinarian literally means *one who uses feet to lead us*. It depicts the idea of one taking us by the hand and leading us step by step. That is what the law does: it leads us to the place where we see our need for a Savior (Romans 7:7-12).

Our need for a Savior revealed by the law is explained and

described in the Gospel. Augustine once said, "The Old Covenant is revealed in the New, and the New Covenant is veiled in the Old." Another Bible teacher quipped, "The New is in the Old contained, while the Old is in the New explained." Back to our beginning questions. Let's take them one by one to see if we can now give the answers.

1. If no one can keep the law perfectly, why was the law given?

Just because no person apart from the help of the Holy Spirit can obey God's will consistently and completely, this does not mean that the law itself which sets the high standard of God is bad. It provides a goal for us so that we know in which direction to go. It provides boundaries for us so that we know when we are straying. It shows us our need for God's forgiveness, mercy, and help. As said earlier, it can lead us to Christ.

2. If we are saved by grace and not by keeping the law, why do we need to study the law?

The law reveals the character, mind, and heart of God. By studying it, we come to know God better and better. We do not have to guess at what pleases Him because the law explains such things. So, even though we are not brought into God's family through perfect obedience to the law but by the blood of Jesus, we can still be helped by studying its requirements.

3. When Jesus died on the cross, didn't the day of the law cease and the day of grace begin?

In the sense that Christians do not have to keep the ceremonial, dietary, or civil laws of the Jews to please God, this is true. But Jesus said that He had not come to abolish or destroy the law, but to fulfill it (Matthew 5:17). As far as the Ten Commandments are concerned, they are still the righteous commands of God for all of us to follow. They are the eternal moral laws of God and, if anything, Jesus made them even more binding when He came. Remember the earlier individual chapters of each? On the Sixth Commandment, for example, Jesus said that not only are we to do no murder, but we are also not even to hate another secretly in our hearts. Paul explained the whole of Scripture's value in his statement in 2 Timothy 3:16 and 17: *"All Scripture is given by inspiration of God, and is profitable for doctrine, for reproof, for correction, for instruction in righteousness, that the man of God may be complete, thoroughly equipped for every good work."*

In summary of our study of the Ten Commandments we have noted first that the gospel of Christ completes the Ten Commandments.

While the commandments expose our weakness and inability to consistently walk in righteousness, they still effectively point us to the gospel of Jesus Christ.

Through Christ we find forgiveness, but more than that, we receive the Holy Spirit's empowerment to live in obedience to God's commands. As Paul wrote, *"For God has done what the law, weakened by the flesh, could not do: by sending His own Son in the likeness of sinful flesh, and to deal with sin, He condemned sin in the flesh, so that the just requirements of the law might be fulfilled in us, who walk not according to the flesh but according to the Spirit"* (Romans 8:3,4; emphasis added).

Finally, let me declare that the Decalogue will always be God's standard for moral righteousness. Moral collapse comes to every nation which ignores these commandments. Life will just not work by any other plan!

The Chicago Tribune carried a story that spoke to me about the current modern crisis involving the Ten Commandments. They reported that roughly six hundred lighted plastic buoys line the Fox River and Chain o' Lakes waterways in northern Illinois. Yet not one buoy is expected to last for the entire season. Why? Officials say that these boundary markers are deliberately smashed to pieces by vandals. This, to me, seems almost unbelievable because as the *Tribune* writer states the buoys are there "to provide safety and direction for boaters." He continued to explain, "Some mark no-wake zones where power boaters must go at slower speeds, [some] delineate shallow areas where boating could be dangerous, and [some] show the way to mouths of channels." In light of this, why would a boater smash a buoy just for laughs? The answer must be that the vandals are ignorant and foolish—arrogantly and thoughtlessly unaware that these buoys were put there for the safety and direction of themselves as well as others. The one thousand dollar fine for willfully destroying a buoy is apparently not much of a deterrent.

This report reminded me of the foolish attitude many have toward the Ten Commandments. God placed them in our lives to direct us in the most safe and satisfying way. They were put here to keep us from wrecking our lives, to enhance our journey with joy and peace instead of collision and conflict, and to bring us to the harbor of Christ where we can find salvation and eternal rest. Are we among those who are foolish enough to break the commandments that would keep us from distress and disaster?

> **If we will obey the wonderful directions of God, like those few who use the buoyed path without harming the protective lights, we will be blessed by their protective power and leave a "lighted" way for those who follow after.**

It is time for individuals, families, churches, and nations to wake up to the eternal value of the Ten Commandments. They are indeed God's lamp for our feet and His clear light for our paths! They still work!

Endnotes

[1]J.Ellsworth Kalas, *The Ten Commandments from the Backside* (Abingdon Press: Nashville,1998) 17.

[2]Kalas 26.

[3]Jack Canfield and Mark Victor Hansen, *Chicken Soup for the Soul* (Deerfield Beach, Florida: Health Communications, Inc., 1993) 74.

[4]Sherri Richards, "Sexy 'Temptation Island' Offers Endless Buffet of Flesh, Stupidity," *The Daily Mississippian* 16 January 2001: Arts and Life 11.

[5]Craig Brian Larson, *Choice Contemporay Stories and Illustrations for Preachers, Teachers and Writers* (Baker Books, 1998) 117.

[6]David Jeremiah, *What the Bible Says about Angels,* (Multnomah Books, 1996)51.

[7]Clovis Chappel, *Ten Rules for Living,* (Abingdon-Cokesbury Press, Nashville, 1938) 42.

[8]From a sermon by David Seamands.

[9]Kalas 58.

[10]Kalas 54.

[11]Jack Zipes, *The Complete Fairy Tales of the Brothers Grimm,* (Bantam Books, Inc., 1987) 288, #78

[12]Kalas 81.